Why is My Office a Pain in My ___?

Naomi Abrams, OTD, OTR/L, CEAS

D1596931

NAOE Publishing

This publication is designed to provide accurate and authoritative information in regard to the subject matter covered. It is sold with the understanding that the publisher and author are not engaged in rendering legal, accounting, medical or other professional services. If medical advice or other expert assistance is required, the service of a competent professional should be sought.

Published by NAOE Publications

Rockville, Maryland

Cover design and illustration by Mark Martel
Layout and editing by Rie Langdon

ISBN: 978-0-9839582-0-8

Contents

Introduction

Ouch!

Once upon a time, in a land far, far away (well, okay, Pittsburgh, Pennsylvania was only 4 hours away...but have you driven on the Pennsylvania Turnpike recently?) there lived a graduate occupational therapy student learning how to take care of everyone who needed her. She learned to help people who could no longer take care of themselves. She learned how to teach children to use play to develop motor skills. She learned how to rehabilitate a stiff finger joint after a fracture. And, in the process, she gave herself wrist pain, thumb pain, and elbow pain. How?

Well, the monthly commute back and forth from Pittsburgh to Rockville, Maryland (family beckons), coupled with the typing and writing demands of a master's thesis put so much strain on her thumb joint and hand nerves that they started to scream at her. She couldn't drive without pain. She couldn't type or write without pain, which makes writing a master's thesis a bit difficult, to say the least.

Yup, that was me. Graduate school did me in. Don't get me wrong—I learned all about how to treat all of these pains as part of my studies to become an occupational therapist. Treatment for the symptoms was taught methodically, by rote: do this first, that second, and so on. So, I tried to treat myself based on the teachers' sage advice. I went to the local pharmacy and bought a brace. I iced my wrists every night. I did my stretches.

The pain didn't go away.

It seemed like every time I got the pain to retreat, it would come back with full vengeance as soon as I spent a full evening at the keyboard or drove home. Another class taught me about this thing called "ergonomics." By setting up my workstation according to a diagram they gave me, the pain should go away, right? I even went out and bought something called an "ergonomic wrist rest." After all, the manufacturers said that it was ergonomic and therefore, it must be good for me. I begged it to help me.

Eventually, I managed to make it through school. At that point, I told myself I would learn all the tricks I could on how to keep the pain at bay. That is where my journey began. I found out that there is an actual field of ergonomics that occupational therapists can specialize in. There was so much more to learn.

While occupational therapists (OTs) and physical therapists (PTs) are some the best people you could see to solve your aches and pains, we don't know everything about everything all the time. (Yes, we freely admit that.) Many OTs and PTs know how to treat these types of injuries. In fact, many OTs and PTs know the basics of ergonomics. However, their training stops after the basics. I wanted more than that.

After all that trouble in graduate school, I became the out-patient expert on the treatment of repetitive strain and work-related injuries. Doctors would send patients to me who already had failed with other treatments in other clinics and with other professionals. *Fix him*! would be written on the prescription. And, not to toot my own horn, but—*I did*. I could get rid of or greatly reduce the pain.

How? I wouldn't let the patients continue to do what was causing the injury in the first place. I taught them how to use the equipment they had, stop looking for new gadgets that don't help, and how to buy the equipment that *does* help. *Work smarter, not harder* was always my game plan.

Everything you read in this book is based on research that I have done or found in peer-reviewed journals. I have put a list of those references at the end of the book for you in case you want to check my facts.

Ready to learn how to stop hurting yourself every time you sit down to work?

Then let's get started!

Chapter 1: Getting Started

First, a few basic ground rules to get us all started at the same place.

Rule #1: You have control over inanimate objects!

The statements I hear the most when I go into people's offices are: "I don't know how [*insert office equipment*] got there," or, "My [*insert office equipment*] just ends up there by the end of the day." I also hear "I bought this, and this, and this, and they haven't fixed anything."

It is true, your workstation does have some control over you. It can "tell" you how to sit, work, rest, and even interact with people. If your monitor is too far away, you are going to lean towards it. If your chair is really low, you are going to have to reach up for things. Basically, we have gotten into the habit of conforming ourselves to fit the equipment and thus have given the equipment power over us. If the equipment doesn't fix things, we buy something else.

However, we can both agree that you are smarter than your chair, keyboard, and mouse, not to mention a great deal more important. So you are allowed to put your equipment in a location that encourages you to sit properly, work well, and be comfortable. You are allowed to be picky about what you buy.

You probably have heard a number of different people tell you quite a few different ways to set up your office. You probably have found any number of fancy diagrams illustrating what you should look like at the computer. If you have spent any time on the Internet, you most likely have become cross-eyed with all the advice out there.

Don't worry, we'll work through all that. I'll help you adjust your office properly. Well, you have to do the actual moving: this is a book, after all. If you will agree to take control and move the inanimate objects back if they somehow rearrange themselves as the day progresses, you too can have an office that doesn't cause you pain by the end of the day.

Rule #2: Wiggle!

No matter how well you set yourself up, no matter how good your chair is, no matter how good your keyboard is, you must move frequently throughout the day. Remember when I said that you were in control of how you work? Well, that includes how long you sit still, staring at the screen.

As you sit still throughout the day, the muscles that keep you from falling off your chair and the muscles and flesh in your butt (the very ones you are sitting on) are not getting a large supply of fresh blood. Your body relies on movement to circulate fresh blood.

In essence, your body is circulating less fuel and oxygen to the areas that need it most. In fact, many people have lower respiratory rates while concentrating on a hard task. Most of my clients report that they move around approximately every two hours. That means that while they are sitting there for two hours the only things moving are their eyes, their fingers, and some involuntary movements of the diaphragm and heart (thank goodness).

You are asking your body to work even though you are denying it vital nutrients. Try holding your breath for two hours and see how much work you get done!

Okay, so what do I mean by "wiggle?"

I'm sure you have heard that you are supposed to stretch a lot while at the computer. Research isn't conclusive about how often you should stretch, but that doesn't stop the experts from telling you to do it. In fact, there are a number of computer programs out there that will pop up during the day and give you actual stretches to do. I find that most people ignore that prompt after a while, but if you think it may help you, just search the web for 'computer stretch break software'. No, I can't tell you which piece of equipment is *the best*—I don't endorse any products. I can only tell you what you need to look for to get the best results[1].

What I want you to learn is a little more basic than a set stretching program. All I want you to do is move: move your butt, move your neck, move your fingers, move your back. If you start listening to your body, believe it or not, it will start telling you what

---

[1] *Throughout this book I will make references to styles of equipment. I need you to remember that my goal here is to help you understand the qualities and features of equipment that is right for you. If I give you brands or websites you might then think that a particular brand is "the best." I promise to tell you how to find equipment—but since every body has different needs, I won't ruin my objectivity, or yours, by naming names.*

it wants. As something feels tight or stiff or even just bored, I want you to take those messages and turn them into what I call "wiggles."

Let's try one of my favorite wiggles[2]. (Look for these **Wiggle Breaks!** throughout the book.)

Wiggle Break!

What I want you to do right now is put your arms up over your head, stick your chest out, look up towards the ceiling, and give a really big yawn. No, don't put the book down—you aren't finished with it yet. Feel any better? Yawning is one of my favorite wiggles. It brings blood and oxygen to the body, stretches the muscles that are tight, and compresses the muscles that have been stretched.

Now, let's analyze what you just did. You have been looking down at a book for at least a few minutes. And before that, you were probably looking at a computer typing away on e-mail or Facebook. Most of the things we do during our day are forward of our bodies. All you did was the opposite of what you normally do. Yup, it really is that simple.

The "rule" for wiggles is that I want you to do something that is opposite to what you have been doing. If you have been doing something with your hands in front of you, put them behind you. If you have been doing something with your knees bent, stretch them out.

---

[2] *Well, my attorney is looking over my shoulder… please remember to complete only those stretches or wiggles that don't hurt, remember not to move in a way your doctor has told you not to, or otherwise exceed your body's tolerances. In other words, don't hurt yourself— got it?!*

Wiggle Break!

This reminds me of another great stretch for all of us who sit too much of our day: the heel push. Here's what you do:

1. Sit up tall in your seat,
2. straighten one knee so that your leg is sticking out fairly straight, then
3. bend your foot so that your toes are pulling back towards you— at this point it should look like you are sticking your heel out as far as your leg will take it.
4. Need a little more stretch? Keep your butt pointed behind you (no pun intended) and lean toward your toes.

You should feel a pull running right up the back of your leg. Doesn't that feel wonderful?

Part two of this wiggle rule is to alternate how you work. Did you know that there is no rule out there that states that you have to work *sitting* at your computer? You do so much more than typing and using a mouse all day. Most people have to read, make phone calls, talk to co-workers, go to meetings, and generally do things that do not require the computer. Rejoice! These are the moments you get to break the chains and change your working position.

There are at least four working positions you can use throughout your day: sitting, standing, walking, and reclining. We are going to deal with each as we move through the book.

Just keep this in mind—no matter how good your equipment is, no matter how well you set yourself up at the computer, no matter how well you budget your time and deal with daily stressors—if you don't change positions often and wiggle, you won't be comfortable by the end of the day.

How comfortable are you really? The questionnaire on the next page is a measure of how much discomfort you feel when working. Mark the body picture with all the places that ache, hurt, stab, shoot, radiate, burn, or just plain don't feel good. Then go down to the bottom and mark how bad the discomfort is using the scale provided. Mark zero if nothing is uncomfortable and you are reading this book to prevent anything from happening. Ten means that you think you should be in the hospital on strong pain medication[3]. Most people are somewhere in between.

Bonus: There is another copy of this questionnaire at the end of this book. Two weeks after you have made changes to your workstation and work style, come back and re-do the questionnaire. If you don't see any improvement, please do not recommend this book to anyone else. If you see improvement, bravo! You have proven that you really can make the pain stop. (And tell your friends. They are probably as uncomfortable as you were.)

---

[3] *If you would call your discomfort a ten out of ten, please stop reading this book and visit your doctor as soon as possible. There is more going on than what can be addressed by ergonomic changes. Come back to this book once you have a handle on the symptoms and then I can help you keep them under control.*

On the body diagram below, please indicate where your discomfort is located at the present time or within the last week.

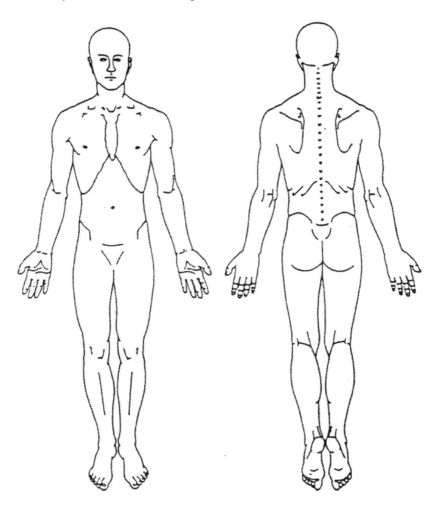

Circle the number that best describes the amount of discomfort you are in. Zero is experiencing no discomfort at all and 10 is experiencing the worst discomfort you have ever felt in your life.

No Discomfort 0 1 2 3 4 5 6 7 8 9 10 Worst Discomfort Possible

Recap:

Rule #1: You have control over inanimate objects.
Rule #2: Wiggle!

Chapter 2: Injury and Stress

*If you always do what you always did then you will
always get what you always got.—Mark Twain*

Part I: Your Body

Most people don't wake up and say, "Today I am going to do
something really stupid and hurt myself." However, there are plenty
of people who repeatedly do things that cause themselves pain and
then wonder afterward why they hurt so much. Let me clue you in
to something your body has been trying to tell you for years: it
doesn't like to be bashed, cramped, or crimped. These are all
injuries.

There are two broad classifications of injury that we will address
here: *acute* and *chronic*. Acute injury is the type we are all fairly
good at recognizing. If something starts to bleed profusely, hurts a
whole lot because we smashed it, or if we suddenly find ourselves on
the floor when we used to be standing up, we are fairly sure that
something has gone wrong. So, what do you do? You put ice on it,
call 911, report the incident to your supervisor, and generally take
steps to remediate the situation. Those situations usually don't have
any advance warning and we just deal with them as they come.

Then we get to the chronic issues—that's when people tend to
call me in. Those are the aches and pains that seem to come and go
for a while. Then the aches and pains come, and don't go. We
wonder if perhaps we might want to deal with the situation. Most
people go to their doctor and say "Doctor, it hurts when I do this."
And the doctor gives out some pills, maybe gives you a shot of an

anti-inflammatory, and tells you to take it easy.

Now, if I were channeling my father, that line would be followed up by the age-old wisdom of "so, don't do that anymore." That old saw might rank right up there with a knock-knock joke, but it holds true. The one piece of advice your doctor probably never gave you is the simplest one out there: stop hurting yourself!

How?

First, let me introduce you to your early warning system.

Self, meet stiffness. Stiffness, meet self.

Chronic pain is actually the last step in a very long chain of events. It all starts with your muscles whispering to you that something might not be right. Your muscles start to complain of feeling tired, stiff, or tight. That is a sure sign that the muscle fibers have not been getting sufficient fresh blood supply. Your joints also can start to whisper to you and complain that they feel stiff, too! That is what they are trying to tell you when you get up from the chair and your knees feel like they don't want to straighten.

So, have you listened to your body today?

The nice part about the whispers our body gives us is that at this point the only remedy your body needs is something like that big-yawn wiggle we did earlier. Your body will love you dearly if all you give it at this point is some wiggling and some air. Move the muscles and joints, replenish the blood supply, move out the used blood and fluids, and lo and behold, life is good again.

But let's say that you didn't listen to your body (do you need to hear me say 'shame on you?'). After your body has whispered to you that it needs more fresh blood and air, it will start talking to you more insistently. It will start to ache and feel tense. That "oh no, I shouldn't have done that" feeling starts to warn you that injury may be knocking at your door. At this point, your body may need a bit more active care, perhaps a nice shower or massage—all still doable.

However, this is the point where your body starts to keep score. If you spend too much time ignoring these informational aches, your body will count it against your internal warranty. Your insistence at doing things your way, or the only way you know how, leads straight down the path to injury.

Most injuries that we attribute to office work are really just the accumulation of aches that transform over time into actual physical damage. You came with a warranty—a limit to how much your system can handle, repair, and re-use. When you have abused your body past its tolerance, it will break down. That is the non-technical definition of a chronic, repetitive-stress injury.

Quick Anatomy Lesson: The Weakest Links

The areas of your body that are most often injured at a desk job are the points at which load is carried, where nerves pass through small passages, or where tendons[4] change direction. For example:

Lateral epichondylitis (a.k.a. tennis elbow). Inflammation and injury of the tendons that attach the muscles that lift your fingers and your wrist to their origin on the outside of your elbow. At their origin, they pass over a bony prominence that helps provide leverage to the muscle, just like a rope goes over a pulley to help leverage the load. The underside of the tendon

---

[4] *Dictionary help:* Tendons = *fibrous tissues that attach muscle to bone.* Ligaments = *fibrous tissues that attach bone to bone.* Nerves = *pathways for electrical signals to get from your brain, down your spine, and out to the muscle or skin.*

gets scraped by the bony prominence every time you extend your arm and move your fingers, such as when you reach out for the mouse or keyboard. Think about a hemp rope and what happens if it is rubbed back and forth over a rock.

Low back pain. As we sit, our lower spine, known as our lumbar vertebrae, are compressed by the weight of our upper body. This increases when you move the weight of your arms and head forward of the spine, such as when you slouch forward. This squishes the nerves running out of your spine. Also, the muscles around this area have to remain taut so that you don't collapse, and this tautness robs them of vital nutrients.

Carpal tunnel syndrome. This is a fancy name for compression of the nerve that runs through your wrist to supply your thumb, index, and middle fingers with feeling, as well as the ability to move. The nerve runs through a very narrow tunnel made up of wrist or "carpal" bones (yup, anatomy really is that simple, a tunnel made up of carpal bones is called the carpal tunnel). This tunnel also has multiple tendons and some blood supply running through it. If this area gets 'angered' or inflamed, the structures inside start to swell and push down on the nerve. Alternatively, when you bend your wrist either backward or forward, you close the tunnel off and squeeze the nerve. Think about what happens when you bend a regular drinking straw. You can bend it a little and it just curves. If you bend it a lot, the straw suddenly crimps off and no liquid can flow through. This is what happens inside of the carpal tunnel. The narrow passage can take some bending, but has a 20-degree limit. Bend your wrist in either direction greater than 20 degrees, and it crimps off, pinching the nerve.

Once you have crossed that line from fatigue to injury, more intervention is needed to reverse the path. This is where your doctor, occupational or physical therapist may have to intercede. However, the point remains—you have to stop doing what you are doing wrong in order for the injury to have any chance of being repaired.

Myth-Busting Moment:

Please indulge me in a brief divergence from anatomy for a very inflammatory statement (no pun intended). Research has shown that carpal tunnel syndrome is not caused by computer use. *Yup, you read that correctly. A very small percentage of cases of carpal tunnel syndrome can be directly attributed to using the computer. Most of the cases are actually due to individual bone structure (if you have a narrow wrist), diabetes, or a tendency for swelling (which is why pregnant women suffer from this very often). The reason we see carpal tunnel syndrome so prevalent within office environments is because of hype. The percentages of people who have carpal tunnel syndrome are almost equal in both the computer-user population and the non-computer-user population.*

Quick Anatomy Lesson: Ankles

Why do your ankles swell when you sit for a long time? Your heart only pumps blood away from it. It doesn't pull blood back into itself. The mechanism of moving blood and other fluids back through your body is actually completed by your muscles. Your veins and lymph system, the return flow pipes, sit toward the surface of your body, with skin and muscle wrapped around them.

As you contract your muscles, your body pumps the fluids back up. Swelling is when too much fluid pools in one area and your body is not able to push it back up towards the processing centers and the heart. When it comes to moving fluid throughout your whole body, the most practical way to get it going is with muscle movement. Now, you could just elevate the swollen parts for an extended period of time, but that would mean standing on your head or working lying down. I don't think that would be very comfortable, and it would make working rather difficult.

Wiggle Break!

Want to keep fluids from building up in your ankles and feet? Let's wiggle them. I want you to start tapping your feet. Leave your heel on the ground and bring the ball of each foot up, one at a time, or you could get fancy and do both feet together. Now let's switch that so that your toes stay on the ground and you bring your heels up. This is very difficult with high heels on—you may want to slide them off. Yes, I did just give you permission to take your shoes off in the office. These wiggles are called "ankle pumps." Be sure to add them to your toolbox of injury prevention strategies.

Part II: Everything Else Not Included in "Your Body"

Don't sweat the petty stuff and
don't pet the sweaty stuff. —George Carlin

The second part of preventing injury actually has to do with how you choose to face your daily challenges. Stress has been linked to workplace aches and pains through a chain of events that many of us can recognize. First, something goes wrong or you get overwhelmed. You start feeling stressed. You focus on what is going on and stop paying attention to your needs. You stop eating correctly. You don't get enough sleep. Your body loses its ability to mend itself on its own. All this ends with you feeling pain in whatever part of your body is most susceptible to fatigue, strain, or pain.

For example, most women carry their tension in their shoulders. When your shoulders tense, they start to squeeze the nerves and blood supply that surround your neck. As that happens, your arms and head become oxygen-deprived. They also start losing nutrients (a.k.a. fuel), which makes proper functioning difficult. That can lead to migraines, tension headaches, arm and shoulder pain, hand numbness, etc.

Please note, I'm not saying this so that you can go to your boss and say that your headache is due to being overworked. I'm saying this so that you can take control of the issue. It may not be an issue of where your monitor is placed. It may be an issue of how you choose to respond to daily stressors.

My favorite stress busters are fairly easy to guess—wiggles!

Move around, take a walk, take some deep breaths, shake your body to some music (also known as dancing), or just have a good laugh at your own expense. And when you have completed all that, consider taking a moment to pick up another book about managing your time effectively[5].

Because sleep is one of the first agenda items that gets put off when time is tight, I want to give it just a little more focus. Sleep is important in the healing process and learning process. We all have some vague idea of how much sleep we need in order to function properly. And yet, do we ever get that right amount of sleep? When we do, is it good-quality sleep?

There are a few reasons sleep eludes us. First, we don't actually lie down and give our bodies a chance to sleep for the number of hours it needs because we are so busy doing other things that can't be accomplished while sleeping. I have actually heard a few of my clients complain that sleep is such an inconvenience because it takes time out of the day. Hint: if you agree with that statement, we

---

[5] *Notice I say manage your time effectively and not a book on time management. Time is not an entity you can manage or control. All you can control are your actions within time.*

need to talk. E-mail me.

Second, we try really hard but we still can't fall asleep when we get in bed. I know how it feels to lie there, stare at the ceiling, and curse yourself for not going to sleep. I would feel remiss if I didn't provide at least a few tips on how to get that good night's sleep (assuming you actually block time out of your schedule to try to sleep).

Often, sleep can be hard to find when our minds are too restless to settle. This is where you find yourself recalling everything you didn't get done, everything yet to do, the conversations you didn't have or the conversations you had that didn't go the way you planned them last night, and even what you need to buy at the grocery store. Here's a trick: put a pad of paper and a pen next to your bed. When one of these thoughts comes into your head write it down on the pad. Use underlines and exclamation points if you find it really getting stuck in your head. However, DO NOT turn on the light. Write all of this down in the dark. Don't worry about being able to read it tomorrow. All it has to do is jog your memory. Getting that bit of worry out of your brain and giving the responsibility of worrying to a piece of paper can be very relaxing.

Your body works on a clock, sometimes a clock you don't like, but it is there. You can train your system to fall asleep at a certain time and wake up at a certain time, so long as you keep to a schedule. If you are having trouble falling asleep, try to spend the next few weeks going to sleep and waking up at the same time every day (yes, that includes the weekends). Assuming that you budgeted a sufficient amount of time to sleep, your body will start to recall that it is supposed to be asleep at a certain time.

Last tip, and this is the one people tend to hate to hear: don't drink alcohol or smoke at night. Both nicotine and alcohol disrupt the body's ability to fall into the good sleep it needs. Yes, you may fall asleep faster after a glass of wine because you feel so relaxed; however, you are also introducing a chemical into your brain that changes how it moves you through the sleep cycle.

My website, www.NaomiAbrams.com, has more sleep tips, including how to select a mattress. But let's move on for now.

Chapter 3: The Tools

Before we start examining your workstation and work style, I need you to gather a few very important tools:

A camera. Digital would be best because you get instant gratification; however, if you are stuck with a print-film camera, plan on using up a complete roll. You'll need these pictures in a timely fashion.

Clothes that don't match your chair or wallpaper. The hardest thing in the world is to try to decide where your leg ends and the chair begins in a photograph when both are black fabric. Select your wardrobe carefully so that it contrasts well with your surroundings. You will be the most important object in the picture, so be sure it doesn't become a 'Where's Waldo' situation.

A friend or friendly co-worker. While the pictures you take on vacation holding the camera at arm's length may put a goofy smile on your face, that technique won't work here. You need someone to help with the technology side of things. Now, I have had people set timers on their cameras and quickly get into position. That risks you getting into a position you think is correct, rather than sitting in your typical posture. Just go with the simple solution: ask a friend.

A willingness to see yourself in a picture. I can't tell you the number of times my clients have shied away from having their picture taken. It is worth it! Don't worry about your hair or makeup. Only you will see the photos (unless you care to share, that is up to you[6]).

Myth-Busting Moment:

Why a camera and not just do this evaluation based on what you feel? Well, most of us don't have a good idea of what we do while we are working. You feel like you are sitting against the chair, but you probably don't. You feel like your arms are right 'there,' wherever that may be, but probably they are not. I've had people tell me that they work sitting up straight one minute and then, when asked to demonstrate, they sit resting their head on their hand. Believe me, we can't see ourselves very well from the inside.

A manual. If you don't already have it easily accessible, please go on the Internet and look up the instructions on your chair's adjustments. Every chair has its own symbols and methods of changing height, depth, angles, and the like. Try to locate a guide book or be ready to do trial-and-error to figure out which lever does what. I'll try to add some self-help tips if you have a chair that only goes up and down, such as a conference chair, but I will warn you in

---

[6] *If you want to send me your before and after photos, go ahead! You can e-mail me at info@workinjuryfree.com. I love success stories!*

advance that those chairs are not really meant for long-term sitting. If you are not sure what brand or model chair you have, look under the seat for a bar-code or logo.

Flag notes or Post-it® notes. You need some way of marking pages so that you remember to go back to changes that you can't take care of right away.

Okay, now that you have all of those things ready to go, it is time to get into the nitty-gritty.

Chapter 4: See the Turtle

Sitting.

We do a lot of it.

We tend to look like turtles while doing it. We hunch over (also known as slouching) and stick out our necks while looking at the screen. Not everyone gets into that posture, but a fair number of you out there do. Don't believe me? Take a short walk around the office. Observe your colleagues and tell me if I'm wrong. Do you see the turtles around you?

No, really, take a break from reading this and go for a two-minute walk—it will feel good. Also, this walk gives you a chance to round up the person who is going to take your picture. Go get 'em!

02:00, 01:59, 01:58...

Okay, I'll take it you're back since you're reading again.

I'm guessing you spend most of your day sitting. That guess includes the amount of time spent in your car or on a bus, meals, chatting with friends, using the computer at work, using the computer at home, watching TV, playing board games, checking your handheld for messages… well, you get you the idea. You spend a lot of time sitting.

Cultural Note:

We sit so much during the day that we only walk an average of 3,000 steps a day. That is only around one mile per day. We aren't getting very far, that's for sure. I'm sure you have heard of the 10,000-steps-per-day recommendation from the Surgeon General that recently made big news and increased pedometer sales dramatically. That goal came about in order to push people to get the minimum of 30 minutes of exercise per day that research shows to be necessary for general health. Yup, you read correctly, minimum 30 minutes, just to live! Walking back and forth from the vending machine doesn't count, unless it is in another building and you work up a light sweat while going. There a number of books out there on how to increase your daily exercise and I'm going to leave that research to you. Choose a method that fits your lifestyle best.

Remember the rule: *wiggle!* I'll work on helping you put movement into your day, but only you can make that choice.

All right, let's get busy.

Step 1: Get your picture taken.

Sit at your desk and start typing and using your mouse (or other pointing device). Try really hard not to pose for this picture. Really get into what you are working on. Have the friend/volunteer take at least two pictures from the SIDE. We want a good view of you and your rear end. If your feet can be in the picture, that is a bonus.

Make sure to get the following shots:

- ✓ One while your hands are on your keyboard,
- ✓ One while using the mouse
- ✓ Optional: if you spend a good amount of time doing something else, such as reading actual printed paper or talking on the phone, have a picture taken in those positions.

Let's start with the picture of you typing.

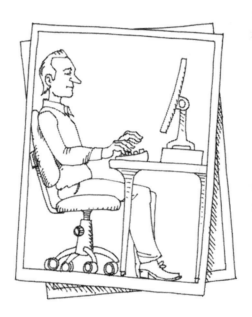

Step 2: Do the analysis.

Part I: Your Rear End

First let's work on your sitting and then we'll work on re-integrating you into your desk. Focus only on you and your chair. Look at your picture.

1. When you are working, is your butt touching the back of
    the chair? In other words, are you sitting all the way back
    in the chair?

Are you perched on the edge of the chair? Are you sliding
out of the chair?

If you are sliding out or slouching down, please scoot back. You paid for the whole chair. You should use it. Now, there are usually some very good reasons why you may be slouched or sliding. Let's figure it out.

2. Is your chair encouraging you to sit back and use the whole chair, or encouraging you to slide?

   Draw a line on the picture from the place your pants or skirt creases at the hip to the top of your knee. (You can just visualize this versus actually writing on the picture.) Best-case scenario: the line is fairly level. If it isn't level, then you need to fix it. You may need to take some more pictures as you change things; however, you will most likely be able to feel the differences fairly well since you are focused. I want you to feel like the chair is supporting your whole body, not just your legs or back.

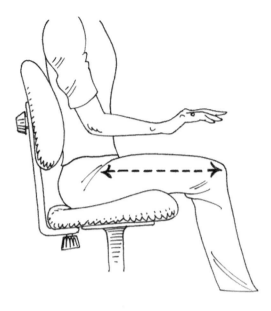

Remember, we are working on just you and your chair.
Don't worry if you can't work at the computer while we
fix the chair right now.

☐ If the line between your hip and knee is pointed
   down, your chair is too high. Please lower it in small
   increments until your hips are somewhat even with
   your knees. If you are short (like me—I'm 5-feet), you
   may need to put a footrest under your feet even when
   the chair is at its very lowest. For right now you
   could get away with using a ream of paper, standard
   or legal size, for a footrest. Legal size paper (8.5" x
   14") is somewhat better because both feet fit on it
   comfortably. This is only a temporary solution. We'll
   discuss purchasing a footrest later. Just make a little
   note for now.

☐ If that line is pointed up and your knees are heading

toward your chin, your chair is too low. Please raise your chair in small increments until your hips are somewhat even with your knees. If your chair won't go up any higher and your knees are still pointed upward, wow, you must be a very tall individual. In this instance, you will have to get a different chair, so make a note.

Side Note:

I had a gentleman I was working with who fit into this 'wow, you are very tall' category. Once a month he attended a half-day conference at a hotel that used stacking chairs. Needless to say, when he was sitting in these stacking chairs, his knees were up near his chin and his back was aching. In order to keep him comfortable we stacked two chairs together and he sat on top—instant booster seat. Moral of the story: the rules I give you should be applied to everywhere you work, meet, play, or rest.

Why worry about your knees? Well, they can tell me a lot about your spine. Pretend you are sitting at a bar on a bar stool. How comfortable are you? Most likely, you're not very comfortable. Ever notice the rail running along the bottom of the bar? When your knees are too low, your body is constantly working, usually at the low back, to hold you in the chair, like a child trying to brace himself at the top of a slide. The bar helps you brace your body and keeps your legs from dangling. Conversely, have you ever sat in a chair built for a child? When your knees are too high, unless you are super-duper flexible, it forces your hips to round and your back follows. Then you end up really hunching.

Quick Anatomy Lesson: Posture

Remember the old song: the hip bone's connected to the leg bone, the leg bone's connected to the foot bone... Well, it's true! Posture is actually controlled by multiple factors within your body. It isn't just how you hold your spine. When your hips roll forward, like you are doing a small abdominal crunch, your spine rounds out like the back of a turtle. When your hips roll backward, like you are showing off your butt, your spine rounds in like a sway-back donkey. I can control your spine all the way up to your head/neck just by changing the angle of your hips.

Okay, back to checking you in the chair...

3. The other reason you may not be sitting all the way back in the chair is due to the depth of the seat pan (that's the part your butt rests on). Sit back in the chair. You should be able to fit 3–4 fingers between the back of your knee and the front of the chair, the part that actually touches the back of your legs.

   Okay, if you want to be technical, 3–4 fingers equals 2–3 inches. You want to have most of your leg supported while still allowing blood to flow down your leg. If that is not the case, check if your chair has something called a "seat-slider" or "depth adjustment" (look on the web if you can't understand the symbols on the chair). If you have one, use it to fix the depth. The controller should look something like this:

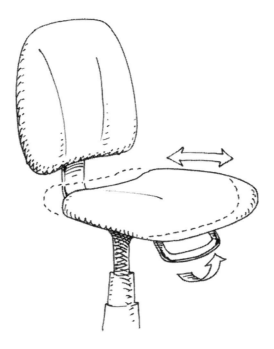

☐ If the chair is too deep, and you don't have any built-in methods of adjustment, you may need to add a cushion behind you. Keep this in mind as you move onto the section on assessing the backrest—just make a note for now.

☐ If the chair is too shallow, please remove all extra cushions you put in there to make the chair more comfortable. I know the cushions said "ergonomic" but remember—it's only ergonomic if it fits you.

☐ If the chair is still too shallow, it is not the right chair for you. You need to look for a larger chair. You can swap out with a shorter co-worker who is sitting in a chair that is too big for him, or look into buying another chair. Just make a note for now, unless you feel like getting up and taking a stretch break while looking for another chair.

So that takes care of seat depth, but if you were paying attention, you may have noticed that I never mentioned seat width. This is the measurement that most people understand intuitively (I think it comes from buying pants).

The seat should be wide enough to support you at your widest width (buttocks or hips).

> ☐ If the seat pan is too narrow, there is nothing we can do about it and you will have to get a new chair. You shouldn't look like your hips are spilling over the sides or you are wedged in between the armrests.
> ☐ If the seat pan is too wide, you may or may not have an issue.
>> • If the contour of the seat pan looks like it has a permanent butt-imprint on it, and the seat pan is very wide as compared to your hips or butt, the imprint may not fit you. In this case, it may feel like you are sitting on a very bumpy surface all of the time.
>> • If the seat pan is virtually flat, you may not have a problem. Having too much in the width department won't really cause an issue in and of itself. The tricky part comes when we start talking about armrests. If the seat is slightly wider than you are, and you like to use the armrests (we'll talk about why I don't like them later), you will get in the habit of putting your

arms out to the sides like a chicken. This puts
strain on your neck and shoulders. Also, if the
seat pan is grossly too wide for you, it is probable
that the backrest is also too big and will not
conform to your spine. Let's talk about the back
now.

Part II: Your Back

You are the most important item in the office. Therefore, the
objects in the office should fit you; you should not be forced to
conform to them. What do I mean? There are two schools of thought
about office chairs.

- *Chairs should mold to you as soon as you sit down.* That's
  Group One. This group tends to use the mesh chairs that
  have become all the rage. These chairs are easy to use
  because they only have a few buttons and levers.
- *Chairs should have adjustments to hold you in the correct
  posture.* That's Group Two. This group tends to use the
  chairs with all the buttons and levers that adjust the chair's
  fit. These chairs tend to come with larger manuals.

I'm a firm believer in group number two.

Group One strives to make sitting easy. Chairs that fit into
group one tend to be sized liked women's pantyhose. Depending on
your height and weight, you're deemed to fit into chair size A, B, or
C. When you sit down in one of these chairs, you don't have to
adjust it very much and the chair conforms to you. The problem I
see is that most people will choose to slouch while sitting, because it
is easy. So if the chair just molds to you when you sit down, of

course, you will have support all along your spine. That doesn't mean you are sitting in a posture that is good for you.

Also, because the chairs are sold based on height and weight, they either feel good or don't feel good. Once you have one there is nothing that can be done to it if it isn't perfect. I'm not saying you should not buy one a chair with a mesh back. All I'm saying is that if you do, and it doesn't fit, there isn't much that can be fixed without buying more stuff like a backrest insert or cushion.

Group Two's philosophy takes a little more effort and thought to implement in the office. However, by having a chair that can be adjusted to fit your specific needs, you can sit comfortably and with good posture. Why spend a lot of money on something that can't be adjusted to fit you? No matter what kind of chair you have, let's look at the fit.

Checking the backrest:

    4. Pick up that picture you had taken of you from the side. Does it look like you are sitting upright, or slouched?

5. Still not sure if you are slouching? Put the picture down and focus inward for a moment, we are going to do the "backrest test."

   a. I want you to sit up military-straight. For those of you who have no idea what I mean by that, think about how you would sit if someone were going to balance a book on your head.

   b. Now, keep your back rigid in that posture and lean back against the backrest. The backrest should meet you before you lean back too far—you shouldn't end up staring at the ceiling.

   c. Once you've leaned against the backrest take note of your pelvis and ribs.

   d. Now— *relax*. Did you feel yourself falling into your hips and slouching down, or did you feel like the backrest conformed to you and held you sitting up with minimal pelvic changes?

WRONG   RIGHT

Check out the pictures of the spine and pelvis from a few pages back if you need more of a visual.

If you are sitting up, great. The backrest is fitted correctly for you.

If you ended up slouching, not so great. We need to fix the backrest.

Fixing the backrest:

1. Walk around to the back of the chair or pull out that owner's manual I asked you to find. Does your chair have an adjustable lumbar support?

2. If you are sitting in a chair that has an adjustable lumbar support, you will either see a backrest that moves up and down and/or in and out, or you will have a lumbar pad that moves up and down and/or in and out.

   You will need to move whichever part you have until the backrest fits you. Use the lever controls to move the backrest and/or lumbar pad. Here's how:

a. First, make sure that the backrest is moved forward enough that it supports you in an upright position. Now, I don't mean that you should be sitting all the way up. Instead, I want you reclining back far enough so that gravity is pulling you back against the chair, not throwing you forward. (If you have a chair that does not allow you to change the back angle, make a note. This may affect your ability to make the chair fit you properly.)

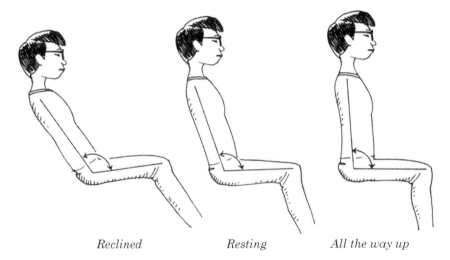

Reclined　　　*Resting*　　　*All the way up*

Quick Anatomy Lesson: Top-Heavy

We are all front- and top-heavy. Our bulk, which includes our chest, stomach, and face, all sits forward of our spinal support structure. We actually look a lot like a "B" with legs. When we sit up very straight (remember the military-straight from earlier), gravity wants to pull us forward and down. We end up slouching. Instead, I want gravity to remind you to rest back against the backrest. You can accomplish that by reclining the chair backward very slightly.

b. Next, move the lumbar support up or down so that it lines up with your belt-line. If you have a chair with a backrest that moves, you will need to lift or lower the entire backrest. If you are using a chair with a sliding lumbar support, you will only be moving that support. Where your belt sits is approximately where your lumbar spine sits. You will know you have it in the right position when you do the backrest test again. Sit up really tall, hold that posture while you lean back against the backrest, and see if you slouch when you relax.

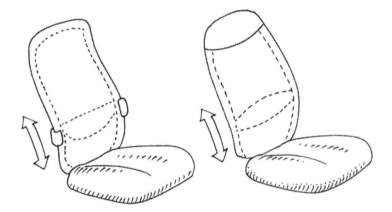

Lumbar support moves   *Backrest moves with lumbar support*

Doesn't that feel so much better? By the time we fix the seat pan and the backrest, my clients are often sighing in relief. It is amazing how good it feels when the chair supports you well.

c. If you don't see any lumbar support, your chair can't be adjusted to fit you. You will either need to put a cushion back there or get a new chair. Here is where things get complicated. Using a cushion as a lumbar support change the depth of the chair. If the chair's seat is just perfect for you (if you can fit 3–4 fingers between the back of your knees and the front of the chair), you have to be very careful with the cushion you choose.

Selecting a Lumbar Cushion:

☐ If you are going to go the cushion route and the chair's seat pan fits you well, I would recommend the kind of cushion that is inflatable. You only put one or two small puffs of air into the cushion to start. Check whether it helps before adding more air. You really don't need much to fill in that space.

- *Pros of this cushion:* They are cheap and fast fixes. They are available at most back health stores.
- *Cons of this cushion:* You have to duct tape it to the back of the chair or it will drive you crazy. Every time you get up from your chair it will try to slide away and when you come back you will need to reset it. I love these cushions for temporary fixes or for traveling. Most people can't stand them for long-term office use.

☐ If you are going to go the cushion route and the
   chair's seat pan is too deep for you (the front of
   the chair hits the back of your legs when you sit
   back in the chair), a cushion may work very well.
   The cushion could help with both the back and
   the seat issues all at once. In this case, I would
   recommend getting a backrest support that fits
   the entire height of the back of the chair.

☐ If you are going to go the cushion route and the
chair's seat pan is too shallow for you—don't go
that route. A cushion will not fix the backrest
issue if it pushes you further off the chair. Make
a note: you may need a new chair.

But what if my chair doesn't adjust at all?

If you are sitting in a chair that looks as if it should be in a
conference room, has absolutely no adjustability and has failed the
backrest test, you need a new chair. I'll talk about how to find a
good chair for you later in the book. Don't skip ahead, though: there
is more for you to check. Just make a note for now.

*But what if I share a workstation and I don't have a chair of my
own?*

There are many of you out there that don't have a chair to call
your very own. You may travel to different offices, share

workstations, or work in a call center where you don't know where you will be sitting each day. This is a challenge but not an insurmountable one. If the chair you have does adjust then get used to adjusting it every day when you get into work. If you have a chair that doesn't adjust, remember that there are changes that you can still make. Go back to the section on cushions. Read on to the section on footrests. This situation may mean that you carry your adjustment tools with you. Don't give up yet!

It still doesn't work!

Don't worry. We will discuss how to select a new chair. However, if you are one of those people who made it to this point and have come to the conclusion that you need a new chair, the next chapter is just for you.

Chapter 5: A Side Journey into the Purchasing of Chairs

Warning: if you did not go through the previous chapters and actively work to check if your current chair may be able to be adjusted to you, this is the point at which you might begin wasting money.

If you made it through the last chapter and came to the conclusion that there is no other option than purchasing a new chair, here are some purchasing guidelines for you.

A few notes about where to go to buy a chair:

1. Best-case scenario: you work with a third-party professional evaluator. This is someone who has education regarding ergonomics for the office but does not have any stake in what kind of chair is purchased. Ask them for references and credentials.

2. Second-best scenario: you work with a reputable office furniture distributor that will measure you for the chair you actually need. This person should be able to provide you with various options for chairs in multiple price ranges. They do make a commission based on selling you something, so be cautious. You have a bit more of a safety margin because they can look for a chair that will be right for you from different manufacturers.

3. Works-for-me scenario: you go to your local office supply store and try out an array of chairs. The benefit of this option is that you get a chance to sit in the chairs and do what I call a "tushy test." Play with all the buttons. Take the time to see if the chair can be adjusted to you by doing

the backrest test (see Chapter 4 if you can't remember
what I mean by that). This is not like a new baseball
glove where you have to work in the leather. Once you
have taken the time to adjust the chair, it should fit your
spine. The cushion may be a bit hard, but should never
feel like it is pushing you out of alignment.

Side Note:

*This doesn't have to be an expensive chair. The chair that I
worked in for over five years had been purchased in an office
supply store. It had been used by someone else in the office for
over ten years, and then was handed down to me when I
moved in. It was a simple secretarial chair that only had two
adjustments. The seat went either higher or lower, and the
backrest adjusted up and down. It fit me wonderfully because
it was designed for a small female—that's me. I used it until
the cushion just completely gave up and it felt like I was
sitting on a piece of wood.*

---

4. Not-so-great scenario: you work with a chair
    manufacturer representative that has been assigned to
    your company. All manufacturer representatives think
    that their chairs are the best and fit everyone's needs. Be
    very careful. They only make money if you buy their
    chairs. They are more than willing to do an "ergonomic
    evaluation" for free. They make back whatever they lost
    in the free evaluation when they sell you a very expensive
    chair.

So, how do you decide if a chair is right for you? Go back to the start of the previous chapter and make sure the chair candidate complies with all the rules. Before I summarize what features a chair should have, I want to finish up the evaluation. Just make a note that you know you will need to replace your chair. A flow sheet for selecting the chair that best fits your needs will be discussed after Chapter 7. (Don't skip ahead unless you want to waste your money—the plot has to thicken before you see whodunnit.)

Chair Alternatives

I feel we should take a slight detour down the road of alternative chairs. There has been a lot of hype recently about sitting on a ball while typing. Like everything else, there are multiple opinions floating about. The research and most experts say one thing, while people who have tried the ball and like it say another.

Group "Expert" says: The ball chair poses a safety concern as we have had multiple instances of people falling off of the ball, the ball rolling away and tripping someone else, and ball rolling over office debris and then popping. The ball chair does not promote good posture since it provides no support. Contrary to popular myth, you *can* slouch while sitting on a ball.

The balls were designed for exercise and it is impossible for someone to exercise eight hours a day. As you concentrate on your work, you will gradually succumb to gravity and start to slouch. As you become fatigued, you will start to slouch. When you get up, the ball will roll away. If you sit down again too far away from the desk, you will start to slouch. Can you see a pattern?

Proponents of the ball-as-chair have come up with a supposed solution to the rolling-away conundrum: they recommend putting the ball on a stand or integrating it into a chair frame. Well, in essence, that frame takes away the ball's instability, which is the sole purpose of using the ball. This modification simply creates a hard air cushion for someone to sit on, which some people find comfortable. However, this is not giving them the core exercise they are claiming to get. Also, sitting on a hard air cushion may simply be comfortable because you end up slouching, which is comfortable until it *isn't* comfortable any more.

Group "Ball Lovers" says: The folks that love the ball-as-chair are typically people who have tried the ball and fell in love with it for some reason or another. Another subgroup of ball-as-chair proponents is the therapy/medical crowd, though this group is dwindling as we educate them. Their rationale is that if you are on an unstable surface throughout the day you will strengthen your core musculature (the muscles that hold you upright). It is true that an exercise ball has been shown to be a great way to build core stability when properly used for exercise.

Their opinion is also based on the theory that sitting in a regular supportive chair causes you to have weak postural muscles. They point to the growing number of obese people around the globe and blame it on the chair. Yes, it is possible that if you sit all day you will eventually lose core muscle strength. However, I don't think we can blame the growing obesity problem on office chairs and we have no research to prove that muscle loss actually occurs due to sitting in a supportive chair. Also, anyone knowledgeable in ergonomics will educate computer workers on the multiple positions in which work can be accomplished and therefore reduce the number of people who sit all day.

Conclusion: an exercise ball is not a good option for a chair alternative. An exercise ball is a great option for getting exercise with training.

Exercise Break!

In fact, let's take this moment to do a great core exercise that can be done on an exercise ball, if you happen to have one in your employee exercise area[1]. Sit on the ball nice and tall. Hold onto it with both hands if you feel unsteady. Rock your pelvis back and forth like you are trying to first show off your butt, then crunch in your abs. Note that I said *crunch in your abs*—you are not slouching then sitting up. Make the movement purposeful by using the muscles inside.

Next, try rocking your hips side-to-side while contracting the muscles that run between your hips and ribs. Again, don't let yourself lean to the side. Pretend that someone is holding your shoulders in a vise-grip and you can only move from the hips.

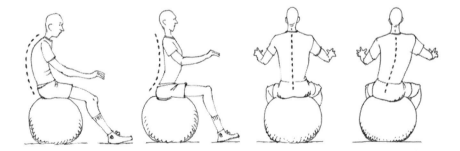

> ## Wiggle Break!
>
> Even if you don't have a ball you can still do
> these exercises. Let's do it now. Just sit up
> really tall in your chair. Round your pelvis
> forward and then reverse and stick your butt
> out. Now try contracting one side of your
> abdomen and then the other to make your hips
> sway back and forth. Give it a try—no one is
> watching. You probably won't achieve a large
> range of motion, but you are still activating
> those core muscles. Doesn't that feel good? I like
> to do these exercises when I get trapped in the
> car in bad traffic. I make it a game and try to
> see whether I can do these exercises without
> drawing attention from the occupants of the car
> next to me.

While we are on the side trip of alternative chairs, let's also take a moment to talk about kneeling chairs. In order to understand this species of chair, we have to take a trip back in time to when we actually used pencils and paper to draw. Yes, many of us can remember back that far.

Back in those days, the "kneeling chair" was known by a different name. It was called a drafting chair, and for a very good reason. The people who needed these chairs the most were architects and engineers who spent their whole day using something aptly called a drafting table. The drafting chair made a lot of sense for these folks. After all, they spent all day working forward, so why not have a chair that leaned forward with them? Hence the drafting chair was born.

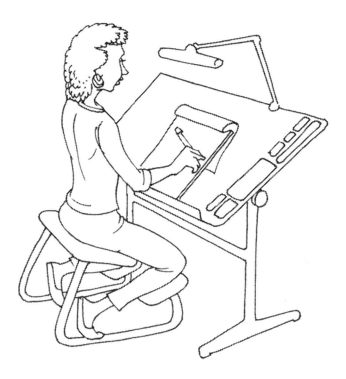

The kneeling or drafting chair has two main components, a platform that tilts forward for your rear end and a padded platform that tilts towards the body for the shins to rest on. I cannot say that this design is necessarily bad; we don't have any research to prove one way or the other. However, this is where I fall back on reason. The chair was designed so that someone could be comfortable and upright while working on detailed drawings: the table brought the work to the person and the chair supported the person upright yet working forward (Rule #1 in action). As you will soon see, I don't want you to be leaning forward. It puts too much pressure on your low back if you spend a lot of time leaning forward.

The chair's design also requires that your knees are healthy enough that you actually can handle spending a considerable amount of time resting your weight on your shins. Therefore, I only recommend that you try the kneeling chair if you can't or won't sit in a regular chair. If you do chose to sit on a kneeling chair, you will have to be very careful that you pull your work towards you so that you can sit up. This means that I want you to follow Rule #3 below very carefully.

Here is a sneak peak at what Rule #3 would look like on a kneeling chair:

Chapter 6: Fitting Your Workstation to You

We have spent time with you pulled back from your workspace. We have adjusted your chair seat to fit your body. I know we haven't discussed all of the chair's components yet (namely, the armrests)—we will get there. Now we will spend time making sure that your workstation meets your needs and is adjusted to fit you.

Challenge!

Before we get into how to set up your workstation, I have a challenge for you that will help you make sense of what I am talking about.

1. Sit upright in your chair.
2. Hold both arms straight out in front of your body.
3. Keep holding your arms out there... how long can you hold that position?
4. Now, sit upright in your chair.
5. Put both arms down by your sides and your hands in your lap.
6. Keep holding your arms there... how long can you hold that position? Hint: Don't really wait to see how long you can hold your arms in this second position. It would take too much time to get tired and it will look like you are not working.

Unless you are one very strong person, you will quickly see that holding your arms straight out in front of you is much harder than having your arms down by your sides. This leads us right into rule number three.

Rule #3: Never lean or reach for the world—bring everything to you!

Let's first look at how that rule can be applied while working on a desktop computer. We'll address a laptop set-up later.

Take a look at the picture of you typing and focus first on the keyboard and mouse. How far away are the keyboard and mouse from your stomach?

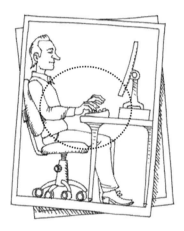

Most people will find that they fall into two categories:

- ☐ The keyboard and/or mouse are close to your belly because you are leaning forward, away from the back of the chair, or you are sitting perched at the edge of your chair, or

- ☐ The keyboard and/or mouse are far away from your stomach and you are reaching out for them.

Equipment Side Note:

Ever wonder how a piece of equipment came into being? When people used typewriters, they didn't have anything like a wrist rest. People were taught how to type on typewriters with their hands floating above the keys, similar to the way a pianist plays on piano keys. The concept of a place to rest the wrists came into being back when computer keyboards were first introduced. People noticed that typists were getting sore arms from resting their wrists or forearms on the sharp front edge of the desk while typing. So someone came up with the idea of padding the front of the desk to reduce that contact stress. This then evolved into the nowverypopular wrist rest.

My question: *Why do people need to rest their wrists while typing?* You just came up with the answer during this past challenge. It is a lot easier to hold your arms out for long periods if you have somewhere to rest your wrists. People were resting their wrists on the edge of the desk because it was too hard to reach up and out toward the keyboard for any length of time while typing.

The first problem with wrist rests is that they push the keyboard further away from your body. Check if your wrist rest is actually making you reach farther for the keyboard and mouse?

The second problem with wrist rests is that they promote resting your wrists while typing. As I mentioned earlier, typists were originally trained to float their wrists over the typewriter keys. This helps limit the amount of reaching and twisting in the fingers and wrists. Not floating your wrists mean that your fingers, which have very small muscles and joints, are bearing the brunt of your daily work. This can cause overuse of the fingers and wrist muscles and joints, which then leads to discomfort.

Conclusion: If you want to use a wrist rest be sure you are using it to rest your wrists only when resting, not while typing.

Analysis of the reach:

Your challenge is to figure out how you can use the keyboard and mouse without reaching out for them. You should be able to type and use the mouse with your upper arms down by your sides and both input devices close to your lap. Pretend your sleeves are attached to your shirt at your ribs. Remember the challenge above? The easiest position to work in is one where your arms can relax.

Now, move in close to your desk or keyboard tray. Can you get yourself into a position where the keyboard and mouse are only a forearm's length away?

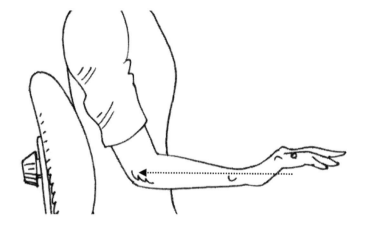

Sticky Situation #1: Armrests in the way

Many people find that they can't get in close to the keyboard and mouse because the desk or tray is hitting the armrests on the chair. Here is where we get into another debate between two groups of ergonomics specialists.

Group A—Rest: People should have a place to rest their elbows and/or forearms while typing and using the mouse.

Group B—Float: People should float their elbows and forearms while typing and using the mouse.

Research has concluded that we don't know if resting your forearms is better or worse for you than floating your forearms. However, research does show three very important things:

- Being able to sit in an upright posture with your arms in a neutral position is best.

- Planting your forearms or wrists on a solid surface makes you use your fingers in more awkward positions and overwork the muscles in your forearm.

- Chair armrests should only be used if they can be positioned directly in line with the shoulders (not out to the side), and only when they can be positioned at a height that allows you to sit up straight while having your upper arms relaxed. In other words, not like any of these:

Compromise: Armrests can be used to rest your arms *while you are not typing*. They are also helpful when getting in and out of the chair, especially if you have bad knees.

Therefore, armrests should only be on a chair when you need

help getting in and out of the chair, or you spend a lot of time pushed back from the desk and want someplace to rest your arms.

Reality Check: Bad Knees and Armrests

A lot of us out there are currently facing the dawning reality of our body's warranty slowly running out. Our knees creak a bit more going up and down stairs. Getting up from the floor just isn't as easy as it once was. Getting off the couch is like trying to fight your way out of quicksand. If you are a member of this club, or plan on working in that particular office for an extended period, consider getting a chair with arms that can be positioned out of your way while typing, yet can be made available for getting in and out of the chair.

Sticky Situation #2: Keyboarding for short people (like me)

Most desks are at awkward heights for a keyboard and mouse no matter how tall you are. However, those of us who are on the shorter side often find that when we lower our chairs so that our feet are well-supported on the floor and our hips have found neutral, we are so low that we look like we are working at a giant's desk. Here is where some choices have to be made.

> **Option 1:** You stay down low. This means that you need to install a keyboard and mouse tray that can bring the keyboard surface down to your lap.

> - *Pros of Option 1:* You don't need to feel like you are climbing up into your chair every day. You are taking control of a world designed for taller people.
> - *Cons of Option 1:* Everyone who walks into your office may lord over you because you are sitting so

low. Your desk may now be so high that reading and writing are difficult.

Option 2: You raise your chair up really high and support your feet on a footstool. Your keyboard and mouse can now sit on a keyboard and mouse tray or on the desk.

- *Pros of Option 2:* You look like everyone else in the office. When people come into your office you are still able to look at them versus up at them. Your reading and writing surface are at the height you are used to.
- *Cons of Option 2:* You may need to get more than one footstool, one for under the computer and one for under the area where you read and write. Also, the footstool you need may be higher than a standard

height footrest, which is a bit more expensive.
However, I have found that many people do well with
footstools made to go with nursing rockers or short
steps designed for kitchens.

Equipment Side Note:

*Standard footrests (the kind you get at an office supply store)
only raise your feet one to two inches off the ground. Many
people who have to use Option 2 require four to six inches for
adequate support. These footrests are available, but you have
to work with an ergonomic equipment supplier, search the
Internet, or work with an office supply company's ordering
department. These higher footrests are often called "tall
footrests" or "industrial footrests" in catalogs. Always check
the product specifications sheet for the height adjustability
(and the company's return policy). Either option will
accomplish the goal of getting the keyboard and mouse closer
to your lap and therefore no longer encouraging you to sit
slouching forward.*

**Sticky Situation #3: Keyboarding for all you tall people out
there**

If you happen to be one of those folks who have pulled
themselves up to the keyboard and mouse and found that the desk
is just too low for you to fit under it while sitting comfortably with
your feet on the floor, you also have options.

Option 1: Raise your desk up on blocks. Just be sure that
whatever you use to accomplish this task is very stable.
Someone may walk and in and lean on your desk. You don't
want the desk to come crashing down!

Option 2: Install a keyboard and mouse tray that has an arm with the capability to come up above the level of the desk. The specifications for this tray will explicitly state that the arm comes above the level of the desk (usually by 2-3 degrees above the track). If you need more height, look for an arm that states that it is for a "sit to stand" station. This will indicate that the arm has a large degree of freedom above the level of the desk.

Equipment Side Note:

*When looking at a keyboard and mouse tray,
you are actually looking at three separate components:*

- **The tray.** *The tray on which the keyboard rests may or may not have room for a mouse. Sometimes it has another small tray attached that is specifically for the mouse. Do not purchase a tray that does not have room for your mouse (unless you never use one). Trays come in a wide variety of shapes and options. Which one you get depends on budget, your needs, and your belly. Remember, you want something that lets you pull everything in close to your body so that your arms can rest down by your sides at all times.*

- **The arm apparatus that holds the tray.** *The arm can have multiple options, including the ability to tilt and rotate the tray. This component is the one that decides how much freedom of movement the tray has.*

- **The track on which the tray slides in and out from the desk.** *This is actually an optional component. If you don't need to push your keyboard and mouse under the desk, you may be able to get away with an arm fixed directly to the desk. Tracks come in multiple lengths. Select one that will fit under your desk. The length of the track will determine whether the whole tray can be stored away.*

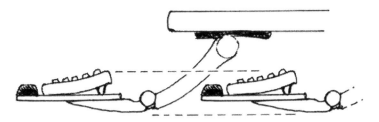

By now you know whether you want to consider buying a keyboard and mouse tray. There are a few steps to selecting the appropriate tray components.

Selecting a tray:

Before selecting a tray, you need to understand how your arms move while using the keyboard and mouse. To do this, first sit up tall and be sure you have adjusted your chair and you are well supported. Put your elbows against your ribs. Put your hands on the keyboard (your elbows should not have left your ribs). Now, swing your mouse hand toward the mouse. Do you see how it creates an arc?

☐ Can you reach your mouse while staying within that arc? If your answer is yes, you should be okay with a standard one-piece tray (a big rectangle).

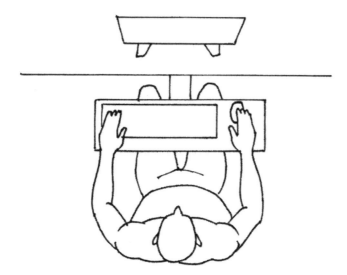

☐ Now, if you are someone who does not use the
   number pad regularly and your hand does not
   reach the mouse while completing the arc, you
   have another option. It is called a "mouse-over"
   design. This design has an adjustable tray
   attachment that puts the mouse directly over the
   number pad on a standard keyboard. It shortens
   the arc that is needed in order to turn to the
   mouse.

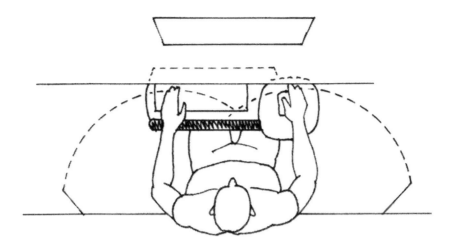

☐ However, if you are someone who has a steeper arc (for example someone with a broad chest or belly) and you find yourself having to reach forward to get to the mouse, you may be more comfortable with something called a "mouse-forward" design. This design has a bump-out on either the right or left of the keyboard tray (depending on which hand you use for the mouse) that pulls the mouse just a little closer to your body.

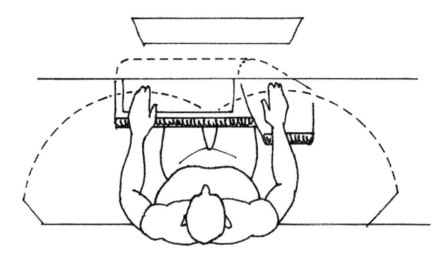

Just make a note right now about which tray you may want to try. Part of the answer will have to wait until we talk about keyboards and mice.

Sticky Situation #4: Can't find the keys

Many people don't know how to type. For all of you out there, I recognize that putting the keyboard down by your lap may be the most frightening thing I could possibly have suggested. This is especially true if you wear bifocals or reading lenses and every time you look down the keyboard goes all fuzzy.

Never fear, there are still solutions out there for you.

Option 1: I say this with love and understanding: learn how to type. Really, there are a number of great programs out there that will have you touch-typing in no time. It will speed you up and get you out of that turtle position as you hunch over to see the keys. Don't want to? There is always…

Option 2: Move the keyboard up a bit higher than your lap and tilt it towards you. I don't mind if your elbows are bent greater than 90 degrees, so long as your wrists are not bending greater than 20 degrees to accommodate for that position.

In this situation, you may have to install a keyboard-and-mouse tray since that is one of the easiest ways to get the keyboard tilting in the correct position. Just plan ahead of time that you are going to set things up this way, since you will have to buy a different kind of tray. You will need to get a tray that has a mouse board that tilts independently of the keyboard tray. If you don't do this, then your mouse will just keep sliding off the tray.

Make a note if you are thinking about getting a tray. The final selection of type and features cannot be made until you decide on what type of keyboard and mouse you are going to use.

Recap:

Rule #1: You have control over inanimate objects.
Rule #2: Wiggle!
Rule #3: Never lean or reach for the world—bring
everything to you!

(From this point forward, you will never again reach

out to type or use the mouse, because your elbows will

be welded to your ribs.)

Chapter 7: Tap and Squeal
(a.k.a. The Keyboard and Mouse)

But Naomi, (I hear you asking) what type of keyboard and mouse is "best?"

The second-most common question I get is about which keyboard or mouse someone should buy (the most common question being which chair, which I hope by now we have answered for you). The answer here is as complex as the answer regarding which chair—whichever one fits!

There are many different styles of keyboards and mice out there on the market. When selecting one or the other you need to take your body and your use into account.

Quick Anatomy Lesson: Hands

Due to the alignment of your muscles, tendons, and bones, your hand is most comfortable in a slightly rounded position. Your wrist likes to be straight, or have a very small bend backward. And your forearm likes to be resting with your thumb pointed up and your small finger down as if resting against a surface. This is called a neutral or resting posture and takes the least amount of energy to maintain. The "trick" of ergonomics is to make sure that you can work with your body positioned in as close to that resting posture as possible.

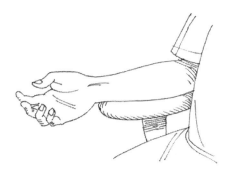

Rule #4: Align your body in the most neutral posture possible.

Part I: The Keyboard

Now, look down at your hands on the keyboard. Be sure that your elbows are down by your sides and you are sitting upright. (I believe at this point that part should sound familiar!) Put your index fingers (your pointer fingers) on the home keys F and J. Now line your fingers up with that line of keys (J, K, L, ; for the right, A, S, D, F for the left). Draw an imaginary line down your middle finger, along the bone as it travels into your hand, and then stop at your wrist. From your wrist, trace the line up the center of your forearm. Compare the direction of the line of your hand with the direction of your forearm.

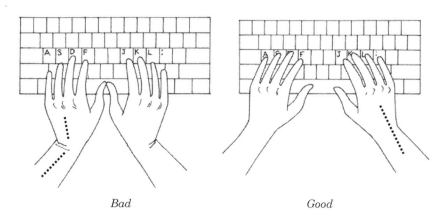

Bad   Good

You want both lines to meet and create a straight line. However, most people will have some outward bend of the wrists. In other words, your fingers are tilted toward the small finger. In medical terms this is called *having an ulnar deviation at the wrist* (the ulna is the forearm bone that is close to your little finger). Best-case scenario would be for your wrists to be straight when sitting on the home keys.

The broader you are in the chest, belly, and bosom, the further out your elbows sit. Therefore, in order to reach the keys, you have to twist your arms in further than someone with a narrow chest, belly, and bosom.

Equipment Side Note:

Keyboards come in a variety of designs. Within my ergonomics world we have come up with some general descriptors to help us communicate. I'm here to give you access to this secret code (tell everyone)...

- *Standard keyboard*: This is the type that typically comes with your computer. It is one straight piece that usually includes a number pad to the right.

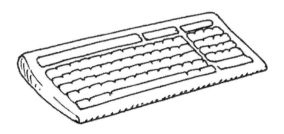

- *Split-keyboard fixed-angle design*: These are the boards that look like they have a bit of a wave to them. Keyboard designers have added more space between the G and H keys to try to straighten your wrists. There is no standard out there regarding how split a keyboard has to be in order to be called "split."

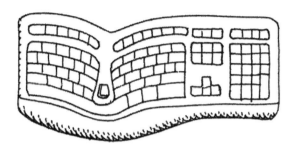

- *Split-keyboard adjustable-angle design*: These boards have a hinge up on the top where you can increase or decrease the amount of space between the G and H keys, based on your physiology.

- *Three-piece adjustable-split keyboard*: This keyboard comes in three parts connected by wires. There is the section for your left hand, a section for your right, and a section for the number pad.

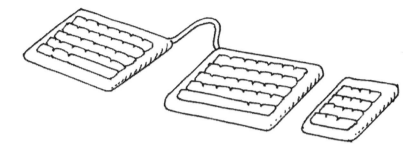

The evolution of the keyboard into the "split-keyboard fixed-angle" design was to accommodate for that chest, belly, and bosom breadth. The split designs are often lumped together and incorrectly named "ergonomic keyboards" because they supposedly fit people better (and it is a good marketing ploy).

The only people who should use any type of split keyboard are those that have a broad chest, belly, or bosom, and have a lot of ulnar deviation in their wrists when they type. However, the fixed-angle designs don't help everyone in this situation.

☐ If you sit down at this type of keyboard and find yourself looking like a funky chicken, with your elbows tending to stick out to the sides, this keyboard is too wide for you or angled incorrectly.

Chicken wings   *Good use of equipment*

☐ If you have a big belly (such as what happens when someone is pregnant), and/or a broad chest, or have severe shoulder issues, you may be more comfortable with a three-piece adjustable split keyboard. This split keyboard actually comes in three parts connected only by wires. You can move the keys that your left hand controls over to the left and the right keys to the right. This allows your wrists to be straight while putting your forearms directly parallel to each other. If I had my druthers, everyone would be using keyboards like this, since they allow for the most adaptability. However, this type of keyboard comes with a price. Also, the mouse needs a home and it may not be on the side that you're used to.

Part II: The Mouse, or Other Pointing Device

That brings us to selecting a mouse or pointing device. Let me say this first. No matter what brand or style you use, if you use the mouse/pointer solely with your fingers and plant your wrist down on the board, you will still have discomfort. The mouse/pointer is best used when your arm does the movement, not your fingers. That is why mouse-pad wrist-rests are the bane of my existence.

The basic premise with a mouse is that it should fit your hand.

☐ If your palm and fingers have to rest on the mouse then it should be long enough to support you from the base of your palm (near the wrist) to the tip of your longest finger (your middle finger).

☐ If the pointer or stylus is used like a pen, then it should have a fairly large diameter so that you do not need to pinch hard. To test this, put the tips of your finger and thumb together and look at the

diameter of the circle created. We call this your
"okay sign." It represents the size of tool handles
that work best for you. All pinch grips should be
no less than one-third the size of that "okay sign."
The more precise the movements needed, the
narrower the handle is allowed to be. When more
strength is needed to use the tool (such as a
screwdriver), the larger the grip should be.
However, no grip should be larger than your
"okay sign."

Most mice/pointing devices are too small for the average adult,
although some smaller women may find them adequate.

Pointing devices come in three broad categories:

- the standard mouse, which is the one most of us are using,
- the trackball or cursor pointer,
- touchpads, which are usually found on laptop computers
  (used with or without a stylus).

Standard Mouse. The first category includes those where the
whole mouse has to move to make the cursor move. The first type is
obviously the most common: after all, one of these styles comes with
most computer packages. Those that are included with our
computers are the ones considered to be "standard." This type is
supposed to support your whole hand. Smaller people can make do

with this type, so long as they set everything else up properly. Your palm rests on the base and the buttons are activated with your fingers. It may or may not have a scroll wheel set into the center or off to one side. If this mouse just doesn't fit, I would recommend trading up to a mouse that fits your hand and makes your forearm sit a bit more into the thumb-up position.

Now is my opportunity to broaden your mind and open it up to other mice that still fit within that first category. The mice that move the cursor by being moved also come in joystick styles where your hand sits sideways on the mouse. They also come in versions with tilts everywhere in-between. Most people would be happy with a mouse that moves their forearms closer to that neutral posture, although everyone doesn't need to go all the way to a joystick. Just spend some time browsing some ergonomic websites and you will see many different variations on the theme.

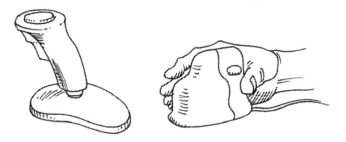

Some of these mice have made their way into a few office supply stores so that you can test them before buying them; however, they have not arrived in many stores yet (don't ask me why). They may be difficult to find locally. Price, computer type, use, and your physiology will decide what type you would make you happiest. Be sure to check the return policy before purchasing since you may not be able to test one before buying! Also, be aware that once your move into these larger styles with tilts, you will need to be sure you are ordering a right- or left-model, depending on which hand you mouse with. Give any change a few weeks to truly judge if you like it or dislike it. You have to give your system time to figure out whether the feeling of "weird" equals "wrong" or "right."

Trackball-style Devices. The second category is distinguished because only a small part of the mouse is used to move the cursor while the base stays still. Trackballs and those little eraser tips that sit inside of laptop keyboards are the most well-known versions of this style. Mice that fit into this category have issues, like every other piece of equipment. These can encourage you to use small finger movements instead of larger shoulder movements. At the same time, they work well if you have a small space to work in and don't have room to move a mouse around.

There is also a new style making its way onto the market that shows some real promise. These are bars that sit inside of pads that would be put where the wrist rests might be. They bring the mouse into the center of the body instead of to the side of the keyboard. This decreases the need to reach out for a mouse. This is a good style for someone who is using a split keyboard that will push a standard mouse too far away.

Touchpad-style Devices. The third category of pointing device is commonly known as *touchpads*. These use pressure over a sensitive pad to move the cursor. You can push on the pad with a fingertip or a stylus. They can be placed anywhere there is room and sometimes are used without a keyboard, such as on a tablet. This type of mouse has similar issues as trackball styles; you are encouraged to use small finger motions to move the cursor. However, at least on the touchpads that you use with direct finger touching, you are able to use any finger in multiple directions. If you use a stylus, you have to be careful that you are not gripping down on it like someone is trying to steal it.

Quick Anatomy Lesson: Tennis Elbow

The most common work-related musculoskeletal forearm/elbow syndrome, *lateral epicondylitis*, or tennis elbow, is not caused by clicking the mouse or pressing down on the keyboard. It actually is related to how you <u>wait</u> to click the mouse or press the keys. The tendons involved in this syndrome are the ones that hold your wrist and fingers up, not the ones that press the fingers down. That translates into a warning regarding every single style of keyboard and mouse. If you hold your fingers in a "wait for it" position, hovering over the buttons, you place stress on these tendons and risk injury. This is a use-and-habit issue, not a brand issue. That being said, I will often recommend that people change their mouse for one that puts their hands in more of a joystick position, with the thumb up. This accomplishes two things. First, it is totally different from the other style of mouse and you must re-learn all your habits. Second, it puts the forearm in a more neutral position and releases some of the tension on the tendons.

Recap:

Rule #1: You have control over inanimate objects.
Rule #2: Wiggle!
Rule #3: Never lean or reach for the world—bring everything to you!
Rule #4: Align your body in the most neutral posture possible.

(Never again will you twist your wrists, contort your shoulders, or keep your fingers "waiting" while typing or using the mouse. or use the mouse.)

Checklist: You, Your Chair, Keyboard, and Mouse

To Buy or Not to Buy?

We have set up the chair to support you in an upright-yet-relaxed-against-the-back-of-the-chair position. We have pulled you in close to the keyboard and mouse. We have either brought the keyboard and mouse down to your level using a tray, or raised you up and supported your feet. At this point you should feel fairly comfortable sitting there using the keyboard and mouse (we'll get to the monitor next).

Only now can you make a final decision regarding buying a new chair or other equipment. Let's put the preliminary decision made in the previous chapter (that the chair could not be adjusted to meet your needs and would have to be replaced) together with what you decided about the footrest, keyboard, and mouse positions.

Answer the following:

1. Did you decide that the chair you were using had to be replaced?
   a. Yes – continue to question 2.
   b. No – skip to question 6.
2. Did you decide that your seat was too shallow or too deep?
   a. Yes – Sit on a bench or chair without arms. Measure (in inches) with a tape measure from the back of your butt to the back of your knee. Subtract three inches. Record that number here: _____ inches. You will need to look for a seat that is at least that deep

or has a seat slider that can move the seat pan forward to create that depth. A seat slider allows the seat pan to slide forward a few inches. This where working with a chair distributor who understands chair fit makes your life much easier.

    b. No – Measure the depth of your current chair: _____.

3. Did you decide that the chair was too wide or too narrow?

    a. Yes – Sit on a bench or chair without arms. Measure (in inches) with a tape measure from the outside of one thigh to the outside of the other at your widest point (be honest). Record that number here: _____inches. You will need to look for a chair that is wide enough to hold you. The chair may be slightly wider. That is okay; however, don't go overboard. This is where working with a chair distributor who understands chair fit makes your life much easier.

        i. Generally, if your hip width is larger than 20 inches you will want to select a big-and-tall seat. You want to have support.

        ii. Generally, if your hip width is smaller than 19 inches you will want a petite seat. However, you do not need to worry as much about a seat

    b. No – Measure the width of your current chair: _____.

4. Did you decide that the backrest did not conform well to your spine and was not supporting you in an upright position?

    a. Yes – you will need a chair with an adjustable lumbar support, adjustable height backrest, and adjustable angle backrest.

    ☐ Check here to remind yourself later

    b. No, the backrest fit just fine – consider getting a chair with a similar backrest.

5. Did you decide that you needed armrests to get in and out of the chair or rest your arms on while you are not typing?

    a. Yes – Look for a chair that has height- and width-adjustable armrests. Some chairs also come with armrests that are shorter so that they will not bump against the desk or keyboard tray.

    ☐ Check here to remind yourself later

    b. No – Consider getting a chair without armrests or a chair that has armrests that can be removed if they get in the way.

6. Are your feet well-supported while sitting at the height that works best for typing and using the mouse?

    a. Yes – continue to question 7.

    b. No, my feet need more support. I will need to get a footrest for (circle as many that apply) my computer area, my reading and writing area, my meeting area, other. Note the number of footrests you need here:

    _____

    ☐ My feet only need 1–2 inches of support – look for a standard footrest

    ☐ My feet need 3+ inches of support – look for a tall footrest

7. When your fingers are on the keyboard, do you have an ulnar deviation in your wrists?

    a. Yes – consider a different keyboard design, either fixed angle or split.

    b. No – continue to question 8.

8. When using the mouse, do you have any forearm or finger discomfort?

    a. Yes – consider a different size or style mouse which puts your forearm in a more neutral position.

    b. No – continue to question 9.

9. Did you decide that you needed to install a keyboard and mouse tray?

    a. Yes

        i. My desk is _____ inches deep. Look for a track that is as long as possible but still fits the depth of your desk if you want to be able to store the tray under the desk.

        ii. I need the tray to be ____ inches below or above (circle one) the desk. Look for an arm that is capable of that range.

        iii. When I type:

            1. I can type without looking at the keys a lot—a flat board or a fixed-angle mouse tray should be okay.

            2. I can't type without looking at the keys—look for a tray that has a mouse tray that moves independently of the keyboard tray. Also, keep the higher

position in mind when measuring for keyboard position in 9.a.ii above.

    iv. When I move my hand to where the mouse should be:

        1. I'm reaching away from my body – look for a mouse forward or mouse-over design. Or, if you do not use the number pad frequently, look for a mouse over design.

          ☐ Check here to remind yourself later

        2. My elbow is able to stay in contact with my ribs – you could get away with a long straight tray.

          ☐ Check here to remind yourself later

  b. No – you are done with this portion. Congratulations!

If you start feeling overwhelmed or confused, just remember that you don't have to do this alone. There are professionals out there who can help you through this.

We are not done yet, but this is a good time for a wiggle break.

Wiggle Break!

Sit up nice and tall. Roll your shoulders forward, up, and then back = big, backward shoulder rolls.

Bonus question: Why not do big forward shoulder rolls (back, up, and forward)?

Answer: Because then your ending position has your shoulders rolled forward which is exactly the position I don't want you in.

Chapter 8: The Monitor

When was the last time you saw an eye doctor?

Do you find yourself with your nose slowly inching towards the screen?

I have to ask these questions. Most people don't put the monitor or the reading material where they actually can be seen. My clients have often asked *me* why *their* monitor was put in the corner of the desk. How should I know? Even more importantly, why don't you

---

Side Note:

I did finally figure out why monitors often found their way to the corner of the desk. The answer was right there. Have you figured it out yet? Yup, that is where the hole is located so that the wires can go from the outlet, up through the desk, and into the monitor, mouse and keyboard. If I were in charge of going around to numerous computers and attaching all of the wires, I would put the monitor as close to that hole as possible. I would be doing what was right for me. So, first thing you have to do is what is right for you!

---

know?

Let's talk about what you have to look at all day. First we are going to pretend that you have perfect vision. Then we will return to discuss reality in the sticky situations section.

If you tend to have headaches at the computer or have flares of your TMJ syndrome (pain in the temporal mandibular joint, the joint in your jaw) after working a long day, read this section carefully.

Rule #5: Put everything you need right in front of you.

People always comment that what I teach is common sense and they wonder why they didn't know it. Well, I have found that common sense is only common once you have learned it. The only way you can follow Rule #4, align your body in the most neutral posture possible, is to follow Rule #5—put everything you need right in front of you.

In other words, your monitor should be right in front of your body. This is the only way you can keep your neck in a neutral posture (looking straight ahead). Try to line up the center of the monitor (usually where the logo is) with your breastbone. How convenient, you have a locator tool you carry with you at all times! Let's put another piece together—if your keyboard is right in front of you like it should be by this point, the monitor should be lined up somewhere around your "H" key. One straight line: sternum (a.k.a. breastbone) in front of the "H" key, and the "H" key right in front of the logo on your monitor.

Part I: In a World of Perfect Vision

Rule #6: Don't bring your nose to your work; bring your work toward your nose.

Now that it is lined up with your body, sit back in your chair and set yourself up at your keyboard. Keep your shoulders back and your head over your shoulders. Now, reach out and see if you can touch the screen. The monitor should be, assuming you have perfect vision, within arm's reach, or 22–24 inches from your eyes (tall people: 22-24 inches is around the length of your shoulder to your wrist if you extend your arm in front of you).

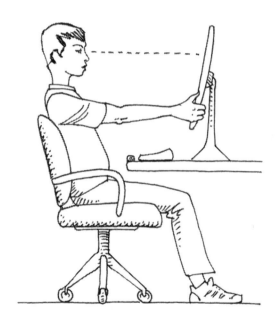

This is going to feel very weird to most of you out there. We are so used to having our monitors out in the next county, that having them close feels like you are being swallowed by the screen. Trust me, start with the monitor closer[7]. If you find that you are trying to get away from the screen, move it slightly backward. However, I can virtually guarantee you that you currently have it too far away. (Yes, I'm that omnipotent. Well, no, not really. I have just done this for a while).

Once you get the monitor lined up with your body and close enough to see it, then you can decide how high it should be. Again, put yourself in your typing position. Look straight ahead at the monitor while pretending you have a book on your head. If you really need the feedback, put a book on your head. It may look stupid, but it does work to help you sit up straight. Draw a mental line to your monitor (this is where the camera and photograph thing works well, especially if you have trouble with straight lines). Your eyes should be at the same height as the top ⅓ of the screen. In real terms, that means your eyes should be directly in line with the first few lines of text below the buttons along the top of the viewing screen (such as what is in a word processing program or Internet browser).

---

[7] *In the old days (more than 5 years ago) we were concerned about the monitor being too close and giving off radiation. The good news is that the new monitors do not use the same components to make a picture as the old monitors. Now, I know what you are saying, but Naomi—I have an old monitor! Even if you have an older model, the likelihood of having problems because of your distance from the screen is small. If you don't believe me (which is just fine, really) sit a little further back and make the fonts on the screen much, much bigger.*

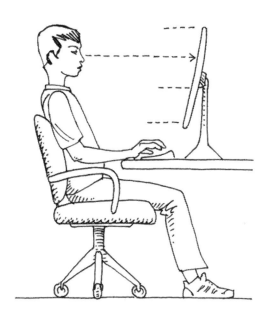

If you are one of those people who have moved on from just having one monitor to having two or more, you have a few more questions to ask yourself.

1. Do you have one monitor that you use a lot more than the other?

2. Do you have one monitor that you tend to use to read long documents or spreadsheets that would flow better if you had the monitor flipped vertically (so that the smaller edge of the rectangle is on the top)?

3. Can you split your time pretty much equally between both monitors and spend half the day looking at one and half the day looking at the other? I don't mean that from 9:00-12:00 you look at one and from 1:00-5:00 you look at the other. I mean that your gaze will constantly shift between them.

The answers to these questions will help you figure out how to arrange the monitors. Rule #5 and Rule #6 still apply: you must have all screens within easy reading distance and as centrally positioned as possible. This means that your screens will form an arc around you. All of the monitors should be somewhere in that easy-reach area.

If you have one monitor that you look at most often, that monitor should be centered and the other monitor(s) put to the right and/or left. I don't want to confuse you, but I want to give you a clue as to whether you should select right or left for that second monitor. Recall that I said everything should be within easy reach of your body. If you use other equipment, such as a phone or calculator, the monitor should be on your dominant side. That leaves space for the other items to be on your non-dominant side. I'll explain why later, I promise.

If you have multiple monitors that you look at throughout the day, they should be placed side-to-side (at an angle so that you can see them easily) with the sides of the monitors meeting in the center of your gaze. In other words, put one on the left and one on the right. Where they meet together should line up with your sternum and the center of your typing space. This will encourage you to be shifting your head left and right throughout the day. You do not want to end up with your head turned one way for too long or you will start to have a crick in your neck.

Part II: When Glasses Are Your Reality

It is rare for me to work with someone over the age of 30 that does not use some form of corrective lenses. I don't know if that is a function of our current occupations or health, but the roots of this phenomenon are a topic for another book.

If you use corrective lenses of any kind, please follow this one simple guide regarding how far away the screen should be from your eyes:

> *The screen should be close enough that you can see it,*
> *and far enough away that it is still comfortable.*

Feel free to toss out the 22–24 inch "rule" if you can't see the screen at that distance. If you are nearsighted, even with your glasses, then move the screen closer. If you are farsighted, even with your glasses, then move your screen farther away.

Sticky Situation #1: Progressive Lenses

The hardest lenses for people to work with are actually the newest type to hit the market, progressive lenses. These lenses attempt to give you three distances of vision. The bottom is for reading, the lower-middle for middle distance, and the top-middle for distance.

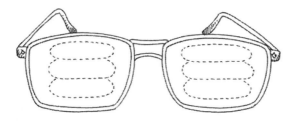

Progressive Lenses Viewing Areas

Therein lies the problem. If you look through the middle-middle (as in straight ahead) which lenses are you looking through? Most people that I work with have gotten so accustomed to tilting their heads back so that they can look through the reading lenses that they don't even know they are doing it.

You are not supposed to use the reading portion of the lenses to read a screen, only paper. You are supposed to be able to use the middle-distance to read a screen. Many folks have to sit down with their optometrist and try to make the center middle-distance lens space larger. Traditionally, these large-center middle-distance lenses are called computer lenses. Sometimes the optometrist will only include reading and middle-distance with these lenses and just leave out far-distance.

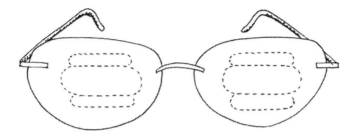

Computer Lenses

You may find yourself tilting your head in strange angles. If so, you may need to consider having separate pairs of glasses for separate tasks. I know that is another expense and a bit of a pain since you have to keep switching glasses; however, your neck, eyes, and brain will thank you tremendously.

Quick Anatomy Lesson: Blood Flow

The arteries that supply your brain with fresh blood run up your neck, along the sides of your spine. They are protected by a bony tunnel as they travel up to the skull. That being said, remember the nerve and drinking-straw image? Well, your arteries are in a similar conundrum as they travel north. Your neck has a nice passageway set out for them. However, when you stick your chin our and tilt your head back, that formerly nice passage crimps off a portion of your arteries. Not a good way to get a lot of work done.

Sticky Situation #2: Reading glasses

Okay, first of all, reading glasses do not belong between your eyes and a computer screen. I say that because of one scientific fact: reading glasses are designed to bring things into focus at 16–18 inches away from your eyes. It is rare that a person puts a monitor that close.

If you are one of those people that can only see the screen with your reading glasses, then I ask that you pull out those pictures you took earlier of you typing. Do you notice how your body seems to be pulled forward into the gravity-well that is your monitor? Once again you have some options.

Option 1: Visit the eye doctor and see if another type of lenses may be right for you. Perhaps computer lenses will help you sit back in the chair a bit more.

Option 2: Enlarge the text on the screen to a size that allows you to see it without your glasses on. You do this by going into the Control Panel. There, you have three options that will make your screen easier to see.

> a. ***Reduce the screen resolution.*** This does something highly technical to the pixels on the screen that makes everything come out larger. One word of warning: if you deal with a lot of graphics-heavy material this will make things look a little bit fuzzier. Those of us that work primarily with words hardly notice the change.
>
> b. ***Enlarge the text only.*** Use the pre-set text options within the display controls. Typically you get a choice of small, medium, or large (sometimes also extra-large) fonts. This will adjust the way most programs are displayed and the icons get larger.
>
> c. ***Zoom.*** Make an effort to zoom into text while working. Screens are getting larger and larger;

however, we often don't take advantage of that new space. Most programs will give you an option to zoom the view in or out. Again, unless you are using graphics-heavy programs, you should be able to manage with less text on the screen at one time.

Note: anyone can use these options to make the screen easier to read. If you find yourself uncomfortable because the monitor just feels too close, try adjusting the fonts and resolution so that the words and images remain clear even when the monitor is a bit further back.

By this point, you should start to have a good idea of what I am going for here. You are trying to create a space where everything you need is right in front of you, at your fingertips, so to speak. In order to finish that set-up we have to talk about the other objects you use on a regular basis.

Recap:

Rule #1: You have control over inanimate objects.
Rule #2: Wiggle!
Rule #3: Never lean or reach for the world—bring everything to you!
Rule #4: Align your body in the most neutral posture possible.
Rule #5: Put everything you need right in front of you.
Rule #6: Don't bring your nose to your work: bring your work toward your nose.

(Therefore, never again will you lean, twist, or contort to see the screen You will have your eyes checked regularly. You will keep the font large and your work front-and-center.)

Only one more rule to go...

Chapter 9: The Documents

For some reason I cannot explain, the offices that have the most paper all seem to be the ones that claim to be "going paperless". Go figure.

There are still those of you out there who have to look at actual paper with writing on it. You do this while typing. You do this while just sitting there reading, proofing, highlighting, writing, or just taking notes during a meeting. We are going to go through a couple of situations in which you may encounter the dreaded paper during your day.

Part I: Reference Documents

Yes, people still have to look at a piece of paper and input what that paper says into the computer. Interestingly, most people don't know how much they still rely on paper until I come in and point out how the paper seems to have taken over the desk. Somehow, all that paper got there. They apologize profusely for their "messy desk." I call it an opportunity for innovation.

The funniest thing about paper is how it seems to move keyboards and mice. Somehow, this inanimate object not only self-replicates but also has the magical ability to shove other necessary items aside, and take their rightful place straight in front of you.

Well, in a way the paper has it correct—yes, it is supposed to be right in front of you. What goes wrong is that the paper then makes you reach in strange directions and lean in awkward postures. Remember Rule #1: *You have control over inanimate objects.* In order to implement that rule, you need to first realize how these inanimate objects work to pull and push you into strange contortions.

There is a best way, a slightly-okay way, and a wrong way for paper to be read while you work at the computer. Ideally, the paper would be propped up at an angle just below or right next to the monitor. Remember, you want to have paper, reading material, about 16–18 inches from your eyes. There is a reason reading glasses are set for that distance! When you prop your reading material up off the desk, you are decreasing the distance from word to eye. The nice part about propping it below the monitor is that if you are wearing reading glasses, then the action of looking down at the paper shifts your gaze into the reading portion of the lenses. If the paper is next to the monitor, you may end up looking through your middle-distance lenses. That isn't bad per se; however, you need to be sure that you don't have to lean forward to actually read the paper.

The slightly-okay way to read paper while typing would be to have it flat on the desk right in front of your keyboard. This stops you from doing a lot of twisting while reading; however, in this position, the documents are not that easy to see. I would only recommend using this method if you're only going to reference the paper occasionally, such as checking a phone number or to copy a few lines.

The wrong way to read from paper while typing would be to have it somewhere on the desk outside of the two places we have just talked about. Travel with me to the desk that represents most of the situations I find when visiting offices and perhaps it will give you some insight.

I've been in a lot of cubicles and offices that have L-shaped desks. Usually, someone puts the monitor on one of the legs of the L, towards the corner. Then, the paper area, or what I call the reading/writing station, goes on the other wing of the desk. When the person wants to type, they pull the paper a little closer to the edge and contort themselves to see it. They got one thing right: at least they pulled the paper a little closer. However, by this time you should know a better way of doing things. Think of Rules #3, #4, #5 and #6. (*Hint*: never lean towards the world, but instead, bring the world to you.)

How can this be accomplished? By this time, you already have moved your monitor closer and can see it clearly. You also have moved your keyboard straight in front of the monitor and down by your lap. This position provides you with some opportunities. Of course, you have some options:

Option 1: The cheap-and-fast method, get your hands on a clipboard or stiff piece of cardboard (I like to use one of those pads of paper with the heavy cardboard backs). If you are using a dropdown keyboard tray, prop the board between the keyboard and desk. If you are not using a tray, prop the cardboard between the keyboard and monitor. The paper you are referencing can then be positioned tilted up, right in front of you. Another alternative is use a large 3-ring binder, set facing you. I'm going to get into this method a bit more in the reading and writing section, so skip over to that if you want to know how.

Option 2: The slightly slower and slightly more expensive version—go to the supply store and get a document holder that sits independently on the desk. This also can be accomplished with a recipe holder or recipe book holder. The book version is a very good option for anyone who has to reference a lot of book material, not just loose pieces of paper.

Many of you probably have seen the type of document holder that clips to the monitor. I can't say those are my favorite because of one very important flaw: you don't read paper at the same distance that you read the monitor. When the paper gets clipped to the monitor, you can't adjust the reading distance based on font size, or lighting. Also, these clips tend to be a bit weaker than the type that sits on the desk and therefore can't support more than a few papers at one time.

Option 3: The more expensive but more sturdy and versatile version—go to an ergonomic supplier and get your hands on an under-monitor-mounted document holder. These are usually metal sleeves that sit under the monitor for leverage and have document holder trays that can slide out and down over the edge of the desk. This is a great option for someone using a dropdown keyboard tray; however, they are not a good option for someone who is still typing with the keyboard on the desk.

The basic aim of this exercise is to bring the paper to you, not you to the paper! (Sounds like Rule #6, right?)

Part II: Reading and Writing

Well folks, by now I should start sounding a little predictable and you should be able to guess what I am going to say about paper that you have to write on or read.

Bring it to you, don't go to it.

See, wasn't that easy?

Slant the paper up to you. It is actually easier to write on a slanted surface than a flat one because you can relax your arm. Just be sure to angle the slanted surface toward your writing arm, just like you would the paper. Basically, the slant should be in line with the paper and the paper should be angled towards you. Okay, how do you do that? Here are your options:

Option 1: The cheap and easy method (I like those, don't you?)— get a large 3-ring binder. I like the 3-inch-plus models. Put the binder on the desk in front of you, closed, with the rings away from you. Voila! You now have a slanted reading and writing surface. For most of you, this will be the best thing since sliced bread. For people who only look at a few pieces of paper at a time, or have a desk that allows for storing papers to the side of the binder and only putting them on the binder when needed, this method works well. Even better, it is a great way to work while traveling with your work[8] or in meetings. It also makes a good under-monitor document holder for those of you who do a moderate amount of paper-to-computer translation.

Now, many of you will rush away and find a binder at this point. (Wait! Don't lose your place in the book—there is more!). Some of you will put your papers on the binder, step back to view your

---

[8] *Want to know more about working while traveling? Watch for my next book, which will be written just for traveling business people.*

handiwork, and watch your papers go sliding to the floor. It's for that exact reason that this isn't a perfect method: there is nothing on the edge of the binder to keep papers from sliding off. However, this is not insurmountable, nor does it discount the various uses of this approach.

This is where your kindergarten art skills are going to come in handy. You will need:

- **Some tape**. Any tape will do, thicker/stronger is best. I like duct tape, of course.
- **Markers.** At least two dead magic markers, highlighters, or thick pens. I know you have them because everyone picks them up, tries them, realizes they are empty, and puts them right back into the cup that sits on your desk so you can experience the joy of finding dead pens another day. Try to get two of similar thicknesses.

Procedure:

1. Open the notebook and lay it on the table so the rings are in contact with the desk and one edge is jutting off the edge.
2. Get a few pieces of tape ready. Just cut off pieces a few inches long and stick it somewhere you can pull them off one-handed.
3. Wrap tape around the middle of one pen/marker and attach the other end of the tape around the edge of the notebook.
4. Repeat with the second pen, lining it up along the edge that faces you.

5. Use a few more pieces of tape to be sure you won't be playing "chase the pen" for the rest of this exercise and the pens won't go rolling away.

6. Take a longer strip of tape and fold it lengthwise, not-sticky side to not-sticky side. Tuck the folded edge up against the top edge of the pen and attach the tape to the binder first. Then press the tape against the pens. This creates a recess in which your papers will get caught. Be sure you don't just tape the pens down willy-nilly or you will just be creating another slope for your papers to slide down.

Go show your co-workers how creative you are.

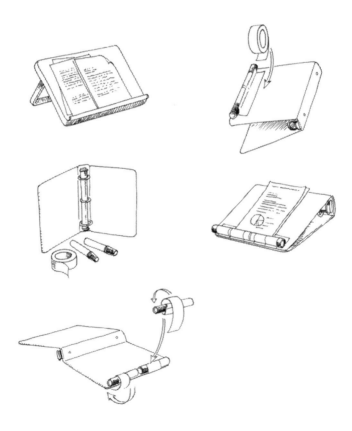

The credit card fix: go to Option 2 and follow the steps to order a professionally-made version.

Option 2: Yes, they do make these for purchase. They are called slant boards or read/write slant boards. These are a bit bulkier, but come with a pre-made paper stopper at the bottom. They all don't travel well, so plan on keeping this one at your desk. It is also important to look for one that matches your needs. They come in a variety of different sizes, from something that will hold one page to something that holds multiple books and pieces of paper all at once and at various angles. Remember, sometimes bigger isn't better. This has to go on your desk after all. Or does it?

Side Note: The Standing Workstation

While you finish reading this section, why not stand up? This book is light and easy to hold. Stand up to read it, and you'll be one step ahead of everyone else when we get to the wiggle that is coming up.

We are going to talk a bit more about standing to work in Chapter 13. However, I'll give you a small preview. Do you have a bookshelf or file cabinet somewhere in your office that gets good light? This makes a great standing reading area. If you have a desk that is large enough to have a section made into a dedicated, permanent, reading/writing stand, getting a premade slant board may be a good option. Take a **sturdy**[9] box or two and stack them on

---

[9] *Note that I say STURDY! I don't want you making something that is going to fall on you, or the person who cleans your office.*

top of the desk, then add the topper, which is the slanted reading/writing surface. The paper should be up near your chest when everything is set up. For some of you, this may be fairly high! Don't want to mess with boxes and boards? A podium works well. A music stand also will work if you are only reading in that position. (You can't write safely on a music stand.)

This seems like a good place to mention lighting. Your written materials need a strong light source pointed at them. The best solution is to have a task light that can be aimed at the paper without causing glare. If at all possible, the light source should be below your eye level. This makes it a little easier for your eyes.

Now if you are stuck with overhead lighting and no way to adjust the light level or direction, it is important to be sure that you tilt your monitor and papers to reduce glare. You still may want to add a task light.

If you have problems with migraines, you may want to wear a hat with a wide brim. This blocks the direct light from your eyes and still leaves the paper illuminated. Yes, you will look a bit funny with a baseball cap on paired with a suit, but it is better than a migraine.

Take All This to Meetings, Too

Let us go into the standard conference room. There you will find a collection of matching chairs that aren't very adjustable; however, they usually will go up and down. You also will find a large table. You sit at the table in your designated place (or, if you're like me, closest to the door). Now hopefully, after reading this book, you are going to change your conference-room behavior from here on out.

First, you will set up your chair the way you need it, either by lowering or raising the chair to meet your height needs. If you are on the shorter side, most likely you will not want to lower your chair to fit you, because it makes you look fairly childish at the table when your chin is level with your papers. You may have to put something on the floor for your feet. I use a canvas bag that looks like a briefcase with an empty toner box inside. No one needs to know that is what you have in there. Hopefully, they won't have too much time to be staring under the table. With any luck, you won't be there very long, and if you are going to be there for a while, you can stand up occasionally for your comfort. (If you smile and warn the presenter you're going to be doing that before the meeting starts they usually don't mind. Maybe the entire meeting can take a group stretch from time to time!)

Now, you get out all of your papers and reference files (we'll talk about electronic media later). If you are using paper, you can very easily store it in a large 3-ring binder, take the paper out when you get there, and put the paper on top of the binder. Again, voila! You have a slanted desk that makes you sit up tall and not slouch while taking notes. This will not only help you stay awake, since you will be getting more air into your lungs, but it also will make you look like you are more attentive.

One other thing that I want to mention about paper and books in general: they land in the way and tend to stay where they land. Be sure that you take a few moments every day to put paper away. This actually serves two purposes. First, it means that paper is less likely to have the force and magnitude to move other desk objects further away from you. Second, the more cluttered your desk is, the more likely you will feel stressed. Now, I know there are those of you who say that you know where everything is and like everything to be at your fingertips. Great, but have you ever tried it the other way? Don't think that I am one of those people who always have a clean desk with pens put away and nary a scrap of paper left behind at the end of the day. Hah! I wish.

In truth, as I sit here now typing away, stretching often and being distracted by the dog (I work from home), I look around me and see paper, business cards, my laptop that I just updated, and other such objects that have better places to be. The point is that an effort has to be made. By the end of the day I take one minute (no more, because I don't have that kind of dedication) to tidy up and put away everything that I can. If I hit a writer's block, I clean a bit. It is amazing what happens: as you put external things in order, your brain seems to get itself in order. Also, your brain works better when you are on the move. There are actual studies to prove that (check out the reference section at the end). So, get up and move, put things away, and see how you feel.

This seems like a good time for another wiggle example.

Wiggle Break!

Stand up. You can read standing up, just take the book with you. (Read this whole section before starting, because you won't be able to complete the wiggle while reading.) Reach both arms up in the air as high as you can. Now try to reach higher with your right hand. Stretch all the way up, onto your tip-toes. Now switch and do the same thing with your left hand. Okay, go do that and then come back to the book.

Didn't that feel good? It took all of 6.32 seconds. (Yes, I time these things because someone among you is complaining that wiggling takes too long.) Aren't you worth a few 6.32-second breaks throughout the day?

Chapter 10: Ring, Buzz, and the Latest Pop Song

The phone, in my opinion, is an interesting contraption. It sits in such a strange state of conflict within our modern offices. Phones allow people in offices right next to each other to take back that "lost time" of standing up and walking next door to talk to someone. After all, if your butt never leaves the chair then you must be more productive, right?

The phone gives us the freedom to talk to someone on the other side of the globe just as if they were next door (assuming you got the time zones correct). People adjust their work schedules so that they can be at their desks when their counterparts in Hong Kong or Africa were at work. Now, the phone is slowly becoming obsolete. No one talks to anyone anymore. People text each other. They instant-message each other. They e-mail each other. Heaven forbid a person actually talks to someone! The only time my phone rings is when someone is trying to sell me something.

So is the phone a thing of the past?

I hope not. But if it does become obsolete, it would open a spot on your desk for something else.

Hmmm... where to put the phone?

(Are you testing yourself as you read along? Based on everything we have spoken about so far, knowing where to put the phone should be a breeze.)

The phone should be within easy reach based on how often you use it. If you use it a lot, it should be within that "personal space." In other words, it should be at a distance that you could reach with your elbows welded to your ribs. If you use it occasionally, then the phone could be an arm's length away. If you never use it, then it could very well be out of reach.

However, there is one twist that few people realize. The phone should be on your non-dominant side. If you are right handed then the phone should be on your left side while you are in your most frequently used work position. For example, if you work at the computer most of the day and you are right handed, then it should be on the left of the computer.

Why on your non-dominant side, you ask. Most people do more than just talk on the phone. If someone calls you up and asks you a question, you look up the answer. If you have to take notes on what the person is saying then you write it down, either on the computer or with pen and paper. Think about which hand has to do more of the work. The hand that is holding the phone just has to keep the phone pressed to your ear. The hand that is writing has a very complex fine-motor task ahead of it. Wouldn't you prefer having your dominant hand free to do all those complex actions?

By putting the phone on your non-dominant side, you are encouraging your non-dominant hand to pick up the handset. You also are clearing an area within your personal space to put objects your dominant hand will need in order to do all the multi-tasking you require.

Something that amuses me to no end: you know you never really multi-task, right? Our brains are actually not capable of true multi-tasking, which is paying attention to more than one thing at a single moment. Instead, we are experts, some better than others, on serial-tasking. Our brains have this unique ability to switch very rapidly from one topic or task to another, while retaining information about the previous tasks. Throughout the day, many of us would say that we are working on writing, answering the phone, worrying about the kids, planning the vacation, and keeping the boss happy all at the same time... but in our brains, it looks more like this:

Boss-pause–vacation-pause–work-pause–kids-pause–boss-pause–work-pause–boss-pause–work-pause–kids-pause–vacation-pause–phone-pause–work-pause–phone-pause–work-pause–phone-pause–kids-pause–boss.

Our focus is constantly shifting back and forth among all of the tasks we have to get done in one time-frame. With each shift, there is a brief pause where our brains switch reference files (we are talking a fraction of time that only computers can measure).

That being said, the more we try to multi-task, or increase the speed and number of things that we serial-task, the less productive we are at each task.

If anyone was every wondering why officials are trying hard to stop people from talking on the phone while driving, this is why. If you are talking on the phone while driving, your attention looks something like this:

Driving-pause–phone-pause–driving-pause–other drivers-pause– driving-pause–phone-shouting at phone-phone-pause– other drivers-pause–phone-pause–driving-pause– phone-pause–other drivers-pause–phone...

We talk about "split-seconds." However, when operating a multi-ton vehicle, you can understand why officials would prefer not to have people turn their attention away from the primary important task: driving.

When thinking about work we often say that we have no choice but to multi-task (or serial-task really quickly). That may be true. However, for a moment, think about what you do when you have a deadline or a task that you really need to think about. What do you do? Most of us turn off all distracting influences (notice how in this frame of reference the phone, kids, vacation plans, and other such items become "distracters" and not required tasks). Why turn things off? So that we can concentrate (and not multi-task!) on something important. Think about how much work you could accomplish if you could limit the amount of topics you are serial-tasking in one block of time.

Handset versus Headset

After that brief jaunt into the world of multi-tasking, I want to talk about tools that can make multi-tasking safer. If you are going to multi-task while on the phone, you have two options: don't hold the phone, or hold the phone and be restricted to one-handed tasks. Note that I didn't say wedging the phone between your shoulder and ear while you use both hands is any kind of option. Why?

Rule #7: Ears and shoulders were never meant to squish together.

While there is nothing wrong with holding the phone in your non-dominant hand, it can become tiring. If you have to do it for long periods, or frequently throughout the day, you may want to consider some other positions. Therefore, you have a few options if you need to use both hands while using the phone or have to use the phone frequently.

Option 1: Use a speakerphone. This used to be a great option when people had individual offices with doors and floor-to-ceiling walls. These days, it seems that open floor plans are becoming more prevalent and people can't use the speakerphone without everyone hearing their conversations. (This never seems to stop people when they are talking on their cell phones, loudly, on a bus or in the bathroom.)

Option 2: Use a headset. There are so many types and brands out there— but I won't go through them all. However, there are two main options to choose from:

Wired or wireless. If you have the budget and don't have security concerns I usually recommend wireless. Having a wire is just an added nuisance that we have the technology to reduce. That being said, if all you are going to do is sit or stand right near your desk while talking on the phone, wired headsets are fine and tend to have better voice quality. Wireless allows you to have more freedom of movement.

Self-answering or not self-answering: Some units now come
with a little phone-picker-upper that will attach to the handset
of the phone and lift it for you. That means that when a call
comes in all you have to do is press a button on the headset and
the call will answer. When you are done talking, you press a
button and the phone hangs up. This is great for someone who
gets a lot of incoming phone calls since they don't have to reach
for the phone every time it rings. That being said, you still have
to reach for the phone when you want to dial, so it can't be all
the way across the room. It may mean the difference between
having the phone in personal space versus easy-reach zone.

Recap:

Rule #1: You have control over inanimate objects.
Rule #2: Wiggle!
Rule #3: Never lean or reach for the world—bring everything to you!
Rule #4: Align your body in the most neutral posture possible.
Rule #5: Put everything you need right in front of you.
Rule #6: Don't bring your nose to your work: bring your work toward your nose.

And finally,

Rule #7: Ears and shoulders were never meant to squish together.

When you put all that together you end up sitting back in your chair, feet well supported, and arms free to move. You are moving regularly and even trying to walk and work. Your work is at an easy reading distance, elevated and tilted forward when you need to see something clearly. And you head stays proud at all times. Got it? Great!

Don't worry; we are not ending the story here. You do a lot more than sit at a desk typing, reading, and writing. Now, let's move on to some of the items that you probably use on a regular basis that don't fit so neatly together. The modern office is constantly changing and you are going to have to adapt these rules to fit anything that is thrown your way.

Chapter 11: Laptops

Portable computers are curious creatures. Though called "laptops", they have never been really great to use on your lap. When they were first invented, they were much too heavy to hold on your lap. I remember my mother's first laptop portable computer— anyone weaker than a bodybuilder needed a luggage cart to move it around. But hey, it had a handle on the side!

Over the years, laptops have gotten progressively lighter, which is good and not-so-good at the same time. At least when they were really heavy, you had to put them on a desk. Now that they are light and small, they are getting harder and harder to type on and the screens are getting smaller, to the point where you have to make the font very small if you want to see an entire document page. Still, laptops are here to stay and I doubt we will be reversing the trend of making them smaller. (I'll talk about the tablet and Smartphone revolution in the next chapter.)

Still, laptops are not the enemy if you follow the rules you have already learned.

Rule #1: (*You have control over inanimate objects!*) Just because it is called a laptop doesn't mean you have to use it on your lap.

Rule #2: (*Wiggle!*) I travel a lot and end up using my laptop for long periods of time while working on reports for clients. I can't always bring my peripheral input devices (which we will talk about soon). My personal rule is that every fifteen minutes, regardless of where I am in the project, I stretch backwards in a yawn. That regularly brings blood flow into my cramped muscles and air into my squished lungs. By doing this, I am rarely sore, even after hours of work.

Rule #3: (*Never lean or reach for the world—bring everything to you!*) This is where the old trick of using a notebook works very well. Think about how you look while typing on a laptop, or, even better, have someone take a picture of you typing on your laptop. The very design of the laptop requires that you reach over the edge of the keyboard and lean forward to view the screen. So, pull out that old 3-ring binder. The only change I would recommend is that you use non-slip shelving paper between the laptop and the notebook. You will end up typing with your elbows bent more than 90 degrees; however, unless you already have elbow issues, most people can withstand this posture for a greater length of time than they can tolerate reaching out.

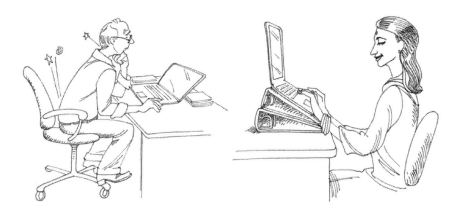

Now, they do sell laptop holders of various types that you could purchase. I find these very useful when setting up a permanent workstation. When I'm traveling, I use the 3-ring binder for dual purposes. When the laptop is stored in my bag, it is wedged inside of the binder so that it has a second shell for protection. Then, when I get where I am going, I just set up the laptop on top of the binder[10].

Rule #4: (*Align your body in the most neutral posture possible.*) Put yourself into a good posture first. Then put the laptop in a location that keeps you in your neutral posture.

Rule #5: (*Put everything you need right in front of you.*) Based on the name, one would assume that people wouldn't have any trouble lining the laptop up with their laps. However, somehow those pesky laptops run away, just like the mice. Your laptop ends up getting pushed to the side so that you can look at your calendar or a stack of papers and then never gets moved back! Just like the monitor and keyboard of a standard desktop, everything should be front and center to you.

Rule #6: (*Don't bring your nose to your work; bring your work*

---

[10] *Want to know more about what to do when you travel for work a lot? Keep your eyes open for book two in this series, which will be about the traveling business person.*

toward your nose.) The notebook will help with this, too. As you bring the keyboard closer to you, the monitor also gets raised up. Ta-dah! No more leaning to see the screen.

Rule #7: (*Ears and shoulders were never meant to squish together.*) When you put all of this together, you end up sitting nice and tall, not hunched over like a turtle. Your ears emerge from the depths of your neck and suddenly, you can breathe.

Stationary Laptop Workspaces

What happens if you are setting up your permanent workstation and you have to use a laptop? Many companies are switching from desktops to laptops since it means their staff can telecommute if needed. (Also known as work 24/7, but we'll talk about that later.) In this situation, you end up with best-case scenarios and not-so-great-case scenarios. However, the basic rules continue to apply. The following options are listed from best to not-so-great-but-still-livable.

Option 1: Best-Case Scenario. You have a docking station that is easily accessible. Your laptop lives in the station while in the office. You then use an external monitor, keyboard, and mouse just like you would with a desktop. In essence, your laptop just becomes a tiny CPU tower.

Option 2: Laptop with Peripherals. You have a laptop holder (homemade or purchased) that elevates the monitor and tilts the monitor towards you so that you can adjust the viewing distance. You then use an external keyboard and mouse just like you would with a desktop. This is what my workstation looked like for my third year in business. It works very well if you take the time to set things up correctly.

Option 3: Portable Slant Board. Your laptop sits on the slant board or laptop stand and you type as you would when traveling. Hey, this is how I did it for the first two years of business and it works. You end up feeling like you are swallowing your laptop every day, but nothing hurts. Even better, you could add an external mouse right next to the keyboard and give your mouse arm a short break from being scrunched up.

Of course, all this is assuming that your laptop is even large enough to type on. Now, as mobile devices get smaller and smaller, one wishes that we had switchable fingers. One set would be used for daily life and the other set would be very, very tiny and could type on those little devices. (This would probably make fastening buttons easier too.)

Chapter 12: The Handheld Revolution

It is very hard to be an author of any material that has to do with technology. First, technology is constantly changing. Also, the brand name of a product often becomes synonymous with all brands of similar products[11]. Well, the same thing is happening in the world of tablets and Smartphones. So, let me make one thing very clear up front—if I should slip and call something by a brand name, I am not endorsing, nor am I bashing, any one brand. (I'm sure they would pay me to do so, but I would hate to lose your trust.)

Smartphones and handheld computers/tablets are becoming commonplace. These days we often sneer at someone who doesn't have a phone that does 100 different tasks besides making calls. I remember when portable phones came in a suitcase (for all you young'uns that is what was needed in order to package both a

---

[11] *Think about whether you call the piece of paper you blow your nose into a tissue or Kleenex. Kleenex isn't a product, it is a brand.*

battery and receiver). Now I'm sure somewhere, in some secret lab, they have a phone that fits in a tooth cavity and can call outer space.

So what do we do with all this connectivity? First of all, we work all the time. Instead of working 9-to-5 because that is when the boss expects us to be in the office next to an office phone, we now work from the time we wake to the time we go to sleep. And some people even work longer than that. I dare you to let your phone ring and not answer it. I double dare you not to answer an e-mail tonight after work. I'm sure for many of my readers out there this concept may be painful!

There is always a way to be able to separate yourself from the Smartphone or laptop. Remember, Rule #1 (*You have control over inanimate objects!*) is there for your sanity as much as for your spine.

Smartphones have changed the way we use our hands and our bodies. They are so small that we have to contort to use them. I'm not here to tell you to stop using your handheld. That would be very hypocritical, since I use mine regularly. I couldn't travel without it and I love my new tablet. However, there are a few things you can do to make their use a little less backbreaking and thumb-breaking.

First, think about how and where you use your Smartphone. We check our messages, both voice and email. We surf the web for answers to pressing questions. We post messages to message boards when we feel other people need to know what we are doing. Now, do you really need to do that on *the phone* while in the office?

I work with a lot of people who are on their phones constantly (which these days is being programed into the pre-teen set). You can be sitting in front of a computer on the Internet and typing something to a friend or family member on a phone. This is a habit you need to break. If you have access to a full keyboard and full monitor—use them!

Now, what about while traveling? I get it; we all need to be connected. However, do you really have to write out a long answer to an e-mail if you are heading into the office, hotel room, or back home? I find myself writing a long message to my client on the road (not while driving!) versus waiting until I get back to the office just because the phone beeped at me. Perhaps I figure if I respond 30 minutes faster, they will think better of me. Often people will tell me that when they text someone they expect an instant response. If they don't get a response, they feel slighted.

Here is where the whole setting-boundaries idea comes into play. I say this with love and caring: don't worry what they think! If someone texts you repeatedly because you haven't answered, they will learn to deal with it. Next time you speak to them tell them that you only respond to messages during the hours of x and y, or when you are at your computer. If they need to speak to you immediately, they can call and you will talk if you can.

Why take this firm stance? Basically, your thumbs were never meant to do all that typing. When you type on a handheld device you are, in essence, pinching repeatedly. I am treating children with injuries we used to only see in the 50-plus crowd. The thumb joints are wearing out, the tendons are becoming inflamed, and the alignment of the anatomy of our hands cannot handle that much pinching. If your thumbs already hurt, you must read this section again! Your hands are giving you a warning and you need to heed it.

The industry is making a small shift and merging the handheld with the laptop and have come out with tablets. These have their positives and negatives. Their keyboards are larger, so that you can type using more than your thumb. However, they are so light that people carry them like they would a stack of papers—pinching the unit between thumb and fingers with their non-dominant hand. Now these tablets have added features that encourage even longer holding times, like movie and gaming apps.

I have also observed many people typing with one finger while all the other fingers are being held up in that "waiting" position. This is the same position I warned you against at the keyboard and mouse—it puts tremendous strain on the tendons of your forearms and your finger joints. Again, your hands can't take this for very long.

That being said, I have one and love it. Why? Because it lets me view documents and lectures without having to drag out my laptop. However, I use the options available to make my body less stressed.

Option 1: Use an external slant board or use the cover that converts into a stand. At least you are bringing the device closer and leaving your hands free.

Option 2: Use a stand and use an external keyboard and mouse. You can do this with most tablets and many Smartphones.

Flashback to the ever-present meeting:

Tablets are making the carrying of large files to a meeting obsolete, which is something I appreciate. Now, use what you have already learned to insert a tablet or laptop into the business meeting.

So we have gone through working at a desk, working at a desk with a laptop, working with a lot of paper, and working with tablets. Let's move away from the desk.

But first...

Wiggle Break!

First, sit up nice and tall. (Can you hear me saying that in your head yet?) Turn your whole upper body and look behind you to the right. Now slowly rotate back to center and go the other way. You should look like someone is wringing you out like a sponge. That is, in essence, what you are doing. You are wringing out the fluids that have been drained of nutrients and allowing fresh fuel into the body.

Chapter 13: Standing and Walking for Work

*(Which is different than standing
and walking **to** work)*

We sit too much. We've already discussed this.

No arguments?

Great, now let's get back to how you can stop sitting so much.

First, stand up. Yup, have another wiggle break right now.

Wiggle Break!

Read this all the way through before giving it a try. Stand with your feet hip-width apart. Then reach your arms out to either side like you are being pulled in two different directions (I'm sure you have a lot of experience with that). Wiggle your wrists and fingers a bit to loosen those up. Once you feel like your arms have stretched an extra inch, keep your feet planted and turn from your hips. Reach behind you and look behind you like you have become a big corkscrew. Then turn the other way. Warning! Only move as far as your shoulders and back can tolerate. This doesn't have to be big in order to feel good. Don't sit down afterward. You can read this next part standing.

The best way to add some movement into your day is bring other people in on the plan. Plan a walking meeting if you just need to hash out some details with one other person. Walk to someone's office instead of texting them. Put your printer on the other side of the room so that you have to get up to pick up the printed pages.

Before we go any further, I want to talk to you about standing up. I know you have been getting up out of a chair since you were around two years old and think you know how to stand. Well, I have news for you. You might not.

Yup, when you are next in public, spend a moment watching people walk and stand. Notice how their heads are forward of their bodies? It is as if we have learned that if we lead with our nose we will get there faster. However, have you ever seen a sprinter at the finish line? She sticks out her chest to get to the tape first. The race isn't won until her body mass crosses the line. Now you need to learn how to stand all the way up when walking.

Wiggle Break Challenge!

You should still be standing up from the last wiggle break. If you followed the instructions from the last break, you should already feel a little more alert and limber. Now I want you to roll your shoulders back and extend your spine upward. Pretend someone has grabbed your shirt collar and pulled you upward.

Next, bring your head up over your shoulders. It should feel like you have a string coming out of the top of your head that is being pulled up.

Step forward without leaning forward. Your foot should end up in front of your body with your hips and chest leading the way.

Now try to take a few steps walking tall. It will take some practice. Don't forget to breathe. You get a side bonus with this one. The more you walk tall, the more you look like you are in charge of things and have confidence. It is amazing what happens when you approach people with that air of confidence.

How about standing and walking while working? The nice thing about standing and walking is that for most people walking is a rote task that your brain doesn't have to think about (except when you are concentrating on walking tall). Standing creates less compression on your spine than sitting. Walking promotes more circulation than standing.

You can stand to type[12]. Many people chose this option when they already have back pain and sitting is too uncomfortable. I like to

---

[12] *We are even moving towards making treadmill workstations more affordable, but these you have to purchase as a set, so we won't cover them here. If you are interested in seeing one, just search "treadmill workstations."*

recommend a compromise and have people alternate sitting, standing, and walking throughout the day, regardless of current discomfort. I would like to see this as something to strive for in the future.

If you plan on standing to type, you need to follow the same rules you would if you were sitting, but skip over the part about the chair and go ahead to the parts on keyboards, mice, and monitors. You still need to be typing with your arms down by your sides with your elbows welded to your ribs. Your hands should still be floating above the keys. Your mouse should be within your personal reach zone. The monitor should be front and center, and up high enough that you do not need to lean down to see it.

Option 1: You can accomplish this set-up by purchasing a desk system that is designed to go up and down pneumatically or with a manual winch. I prefer the pneumatic option because it usually can be set to get into the right position either sitting or standing with the push of a button; however, there is a cost difference.

Option 2: There also are attachments you can put on your desk to make your monitor and keyboard/mouse move upward as one unit. The monitor gets attached to a monitor arm, which is basically a multi-jointed pneumatic apparatus that allows you to move the monitor almost weightlessly. There are keyboard/mouse tray arms that are specifically configured for sit-stand workstations. They just have a wider range of movement.

Option 3: You also can make a standing workstation just like you made a standing read/write station. Put a **sturdy** box on the desk for your keyboard and mouse and another taller **sturdy** stack of boxes for your monitor. This works well if you have a second computer. Alternatively, you can make your seated desk your reading area and your standing desk your typing area. There is no rule that says you must have the option of typing while sitting.

Option 4: You raise your whole desk up with blocks or extenders. Then you can get a computer chair that is up higher, now called a task work stool, so that you can alternate sitting with standing. Remember that you will need something to support your feet while sitting if you are all the way up on a stool. The foot rings that come with these stools often are too low. I would recommend planning on a high footrest.

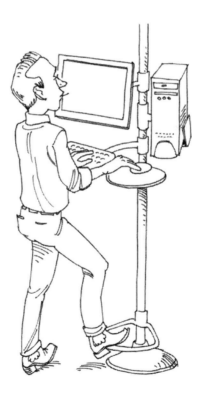

There are two added rules for the standing workstation. First, static standing, or standing still, can be uncomfortable if you do it for too long. Therefore, it is recommended that you actually shift your weight side to side frequently while standing. This can be accomplished with a short step or even an old phone book wrapped up in duct tape. Put it under one foot then shift it to be under the other. In this way, you are shifting the spinal pressures and foot pressures, and will be able to tolerate the standing better.

Second, standing in high heels for long periods can put added pressure on your feet and spine. How about swapping those heels for more supportive shoes for a portion of the day?

I do have one word of caution regarding these sit-stand computer stations. I have worked with companies that have put a lot of money into installing sit-stand stations for a large number of workers. Most often people will set the desk in the most comfortable position, either sitting or standing, and never change it. If you are going to invest in a sit-stand station, be sure you know how to use the device and be sure you can integrate it into your day. Make a plan. Stick to the plan. Either that, or you have wasted your money and I really hate for you to do that.

Chapter 14: Put it All Together

A lot of what we talked about so far really boils down to taking responsibility and having accountability for your actions and choices. True, you can only change your actions so much before new equipment is needed. At no point could I say that every situation can be solved with habit changes alone. However, we jump on new equipment quickly in the hopes that it will solve our problems. Well, I'm very sorry to be the one to tell you this, but expensive and shiny new equipment won't solve anything if they are incorrect for you or used to put a bandage on the wrong problem.

Recap:

Rule #1: You have control over inanimate objects.
Rule #2: Wiggle!
Rule #3: Never lean or reach for the world—bring everything to you!
Rule #4: Align your body in the most neutral posture possible.
Rule #5: Put everything you need right in front of you.
Rule #6: Don't bring your nose to your work: bring your work toward your nose.
Rule #7: Ears and shoulders were never meant to squish together.

Checklist: Every Time You Go to Work

- If you are sitting, you have adjusted the chair to fit you (if you are standing go on to the next step).
  - ☐ You are able to sit all the way back in the chair.
  - ☐ You are able to rest against the backrest without slumping.
  - ☐ You are upright yet able to feel your weight supported up against the backrest.
  - ☐ Your feet are well supported either on the floor or on a footrest.
- If you are standing, you have a short step nearby so that you can rest one foot on the step and shift your weight side to side.
- Your elbows are welded to your sides.
  - ☐ Your keyboard is directly in front of you and almost touching your belly.
- Your mouse is as close to you as possible. You can reach it without moving your elbow away from your body.
  - ☐ You are able to see everything you are reading without sticking your chin out, leaning forward or otherwise looking like a turtle.
  - ☐ Your monitor is straight in front and within an easy reading distance.
  - ☐ Your paper materials are tilted upward and within easy reading distance.
  - ☐ You have put your phone in the proper reach zone (in your personal space if you use it frequently or a little further away if you don't use it frequently).

☐ You have created a system for yourself to remember to wiggle often, such as promising yourself you will wiggle every time the phone rings or your computer auto-saves your work.

☐ Your Smartphone or tablet is put aside or propped up with peripherals.

☐ Take a deep breath.

☐ Take another deep breath.

Now you are ready to work.

I want to give you one more rule that is not really about ergonomics, but about taking care of you...

Bonus Rule: Don't let discomfort become normal for you.

There are professionals out there that can help alleviate the aches.

What should you do if you already have discomfort while working in your office? First of all, do a self-assessment. How far out of neutral are you asking your body to work? How stressed are you and how is that stress putting itself into your muscles and pulling at your posture? What have you tried, or not tried?

Next, do something about the discomfort. Put a cold pack on anything that hurts[13] for around 10–20 minutes. Think of cold as something that calms irritations. Heat should only be used when something feels tight because heat relaxes.

Also, tell someone other than your family (unless you work in a family business). Your doctor, occupational, or physical therapist would be good to speak with if you already have a relationship with one. Words of caution here, if the aches and pains continue and you don't seem to be getting relief, ask to see a specialist. As I said earlier, being able to identify contributing factors and make ergonomic changes is a sub-specialty and requires additional training.

Congratulations on choosing to make changes to the way you

---

[13] *Okay, one more stern look from my attorney and I may turn to stone. Remember, don't do anything that hurts or goes against the advice of your personal physician or therapist. If you can't feel hot and cold on an area of your skin, please DO NOT use these methods. If you have an open sore, cut, burn, rash, or other thing that would be classified as not good, please DO NOT use these methods.*

work! Try this new set-up for at least two weeks. Put on your calendar that you are going to come back to this book after that trial period and reassess your comfort. As promised, another copy of the body diagram discomfort scoring is provided on the following page. Compare it to the one you did at the beginning of this process.

Is the discomfort better? Please e-mail me at info@workinjuryfree.com—I love happy endings. And if you aren't in a happy place, keep reading.

If your symptoms are not getting better at all, and you have done a re-assessment of your workstation using this book and still have not figured out what is going wrong, e-mail me a photo of you at your workstation (info@workinjuryfree.com). I'll give it a quick once-over for free. Yup, you read that right—I'm so sure that things will start getting better when you put my seven rules into place that I am willing to offer you a free photograph evaluation if this system doesn't work.

On the body diagram below, please indicate where your discomfort is located at the present time or within the last week.

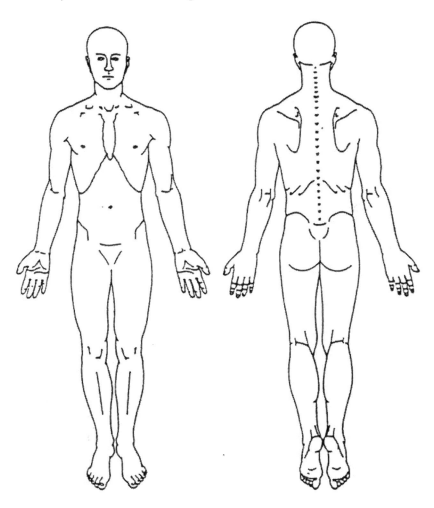

Circle the number that best describes the amount of discomfort you are in. Zero is experiencing no discomfort at all and 10 is experiencing the worst discomfort you have ever felt in your life.

No Discomfort 0 1 2 3 4 5 6 7 8 9 10 Worst Discomfort Possible

References and Resources

Here is a list of all of the articles, books, journals, and other resources I used to grow my knowledge base before imparting wisdom unto you. I am including the list here so that you can have a chance to grow your own knowledge (just in case you feel like reading scientific articles in your spare time). However, may I recommend that you use some of that spare time to go outside and take a walk, maybe go to the gym, you could even turn off your Smartphone and play with the dog. If you don't have a dog, I'm sorry… You can borrow mine for the "awww" factor and the laughter.

Wiggle Break!

Laughter is a great wiggle. (Yes, she really does sleep upside-down.)

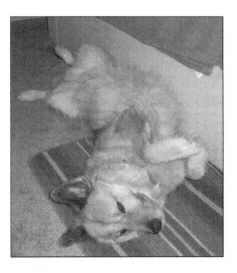

Okay, here are those resources:

Abrams, N. (2008). Sample job analysis and design considerations.
    In K. Jacobs (Ed.), *Ergonomics for therapists* (pp. 397-415).
    Philadelphia, PA: Elsevier.

Abrams, N. (2010). Motivation, communication, and change:
    Ergonomic program success. *Work & Industry Special
    Interest Section Quarterly, 24*(2), pp. 1-4.

Abrams, N. (2011). *Occupation-Based Office Ergonomics*. Rockville:
    Abrams.

Amell, T., & Kumar, S. (2001). Work-related musculoskeletal
    disorders: Design as a prevention strategy. A review.
    Journal of Occupational Rehabilitation, 11(4), 255-265.

American Occupational Therapy Association. (2008). Occupational
    therapy practice framework: Domain and process (2nd ed.).
    American Journal of Occupational Therapy, 62, pp. 625-683.

Baker, N. A. (2009). Alternative keyboards. *Work & Industry
    Special Interest Section Quarterly, 23*(3), pp. 1-4.

Baker, N. A., & Cidboy, E. L. (2006). The effect of three alternative
    keyboard designs on forearm pronation, wrist extension, and
    ulnar deviation: A meta-analysis. *American Journal of
    Occupational Therapy, 60*(1), 40-79.

Baker, N. A., & Redfern, M. (2009). Potentially problematic postures
    during work site keyboard use. *The American Journal of
    Occupational Therapy, 63*(4), 386-397.

Baker, N. A., Sussman, N. B., & Redfern, M. S. (2008).
    Discriminating between individuals with and without
    musculoskeletal disorders of the upper extremity by means
    of items related to computer keyboard use. *Journal of*

Occupational Rehabilitation, 18, 157-165.

Berg Rice, V. J. (2008). Macroergonomics. In K. Jacobs (Ed.), *Ergonomics for therapists* (3rd ed., pp. 37-47). Philidelphia, PA: Mosby Elsevier.

Bernaards, C. M., Ariens, G. A., Simons, M., Knol, D. L., & Hildebrandt, V. H. (2008). Improving work style behavior in computer workers with neck and upper limb symptoms. *Journal of Occupational Rehabilitation, 18,* 87-101.

Bernacki, E. J., Guidera, J. A., Schaefer, J. A., Lavin, R. A., & Tsai, S. P. (1999). An ergonomics program designed to reduce the incidence of upper extremity work related musculoskeletal disorders. *Journal of Occupational and Environmental Medicine, 41*(12), 1032-1041.

Bernard, B. P. (Ed.). (1997). *Musculoskeletal disorders and workplace factors: A critical review of epidemiologic evidence for work-related musculoskeletal disorders of the neck, upper extremity, and low back.* Washington, DC: U.S. Department of Health and Human Services National Institute for Occupational Safety and Health.

Bohr, P. C. (2000). Efficacy of office ergonomics. *Journal of Occupational Rehabilitation, 10*(4), 243-255.

Bongers, P. M., Ijmker, S., van den Heuvel, S., & Blatter, B. M. (2006). Epidemiology of work related neck and upper limb problems: Psychsocial and personal risk factors (Part I) and effective interventions from a bio behavioural perspective (Part II). *Journal of Occupational Rehabilitation, 16,* 279-302.

Budnick, P. (Ed.). (2004). *Fundamentals of Office Ergonomics.* Park

City, UT: Ergoweb Inc.

David, G. C. (2005). Ergonomic methods for assessing exposure to risk factors for work-related musculoskeletal disorders. *Occupational Medicine, 55,* 190-199.

Delisle, A., Lariviere, C., Plamondon, A., & Imbeau, D. (2006). Comparison of three computer office workstations offering forearm support: Impact on upper limb posture and muscle activation. *Ergonomics, 49*(2), 139-160.

Eltayeb, S., Staal, J. B., Hassan, A., & de Bie, R. A. (2009). Work related risk factors for neck, shoulder and arms complaints: A cohort study among Dutch computer office workers. *Journal of Occupational Rehabilitation, 19,* 315-322.

ErgoSystems Consulting Group, Inc. (n.d.). Office ergonomics workstation assessment worksheet. http://www.risk-safety.admin.state.mn.us/pdfrtfs/Office%20Ergonomics%20Assessment%20Worksheet%20Short%20%20Form.pdf.

Faucett, J., Blanc, P. D., & Yelin, E. (2000). The impact of carpal tunnel syndrome on work status: Implications of job characteristics for staying on the job. *Journal of Occupational Rehabilitation, 10*(1), 55-69.

Feuerstein, M., Armstrong, T., Hickey, P., & Lincoln, A. (1997). Computer keyboard force and upper extremity symptoms. *Journal of Occupational and Environmental Medicine, 39*(12), 114-1153.

Fick, F. (2008, December). Ergonomic assessment and solutions: More than musculoskeletal risk factors. *Work & Industry SIS Quarterly, 22*(4), 1-3.

Gadge, K., & Innes, E. (2007). An investigation into the immediate effects on comfort, productivity and posture of the Bambach saddle seat and a standard office chair. *Work, 29*, 189-203.

Griffiths, K. L., Mackey, M. G., & Adamson, B. J. (2007). The impact of a computerized work environment on professional occupational groups and behavioral and physiological risk factors for musculoskeletal symptoms: A literature review. *Journal of Occupational Rehabilitation, 17*, 743-765.

Heinrich, J., Blatter, B. M., & Bongers, P. M. (2004). A comparison of methods for the assessment of postural load and duration of computer use. *Occupational Environmental Medicine, 61*, 1027-1031.

Human Factors and Ergonomics Society. (2007). *ANSI/HFES 100-2007: Human Factors Engineering of Computer Workstations.* Human Factors and Ergonomics Society.

Human Factors and Ergonomics Society. (n.d.). Retrieved 10 23, 2010, from http://www.hfes.org/web/EducationalResources/HFEdefinitionsmain.html

Johnston, V., Jull, G., Souvlis, T., & Jimmieson, N. L. (2010, September). Interactive effects from self-reported physical and psychosocial factors in the workplace on neck pain and disability in female office workers. *Ergonomics, 53*(4), 502-513.

Jones, T., & Kumar, S. (2001). Physical ergonomics in low-back pain prevention. *Journal of Occupational Rehabilitation, 11*(4), 309-319.

Ketola, R., Toivonen, R., Hakkanen, M., Luukkonen, R., Takala, E. P., Viikari-Juntura, E., & Ergonomics, t. E. (2002). Effects of ergonomic intervention in work with video display units. *Scandinavian Journal of Work Environmental Health, 28*(1), 18-24.

Korhonen, T., Ketola, R., Toivonen, R., Luukonen, R., Kakkanen, M., & Viikari-Juntura, E. (2003). Work related and individual predictors for incident neck pain among office employees working with video display units. *Occupational Environmental Medicine, 60*, 475-482.

Laestadius, J. G., Ye, J., Cai, X., Ross, S., Dimberg, L., & Klekner, M. (2009). The proactive approach—Is it worthwhile? A prospective controlled ergonomic intervention study in office workers. *Journal of Occupational and Environmental Medicine, 51*(10), 1116-1124.

Legg, S. J., Mackie, H. W., & Milicich, W. (2002). Evaluation of a prototype multi-posture office chair. *Ergonomics, 45*(2), 153-163.

May, D. R., Reed, K., Schwoerer, C. E., & Potter, P. (2004). Ergonomic office design and aging: A quasi-experimental field study of employee reactions to an ergonomics intervention program. *Journal of Occupational Health Psychology, 9*(2), 123-135.

Meijer, E. M., Sluiter, J. K., & Frings-Dresen, M. H. (2008, August). Is workstyle a mediating factor for pain in the upper extremity over time? *Journal of Occupational Rehabilitation, 18*, pp. 262-266.

Moore, J. S., Garg, A., & Hegmann, K. (2006). *Applied Ergonomics Upper Extremity*. WI: University of Wisconsin.

Moray, N. (2000). Culture, politics and ergonomics. *Ergonomics,*

43(7), 858-868.

National Institute for Occupational Safety and Health. (n.d.). Retrieved October 25, 2010, from CDC NIOSH: http://www.cdc.gov/niosh/topics/workorg/tools/pdfs/NIOSH-Generic-Job-Stress-Questionaire.pdf

National Institute for Occupational Safety and Health. (n.d.). *NIOSH Publication No 97-117 Elements of Ergonomics Programs Toolbox Tray 4: Data Gathering-Medical and Health Indication.* Washington. Retrieved from: http://www.cdc.gov/niosh/docs/97-117/

Pillastrini, P., Mungnai, R., Farneti, C., Bertozzi, L., Bonfiglioli, R., Curti, S., . . . Violante, F. S. (2007). Evaluation of two preventive interventions for reducing musculoskeletal complaints in operators of video display terminals. *Physical Therapy, 87*(5), 536-544.

Pynt, J., Mackey, M. G., & Higgs, J. (2008). Kyphosed seated postures: Extending concepts of postural health beyond the office. *Journal of Occupational Rehabilitation, 18*, 35-45.

Ripat, J., Scatliff, T., Giesbrect, E., Quanbury, A., Friesen, M., & Kelso, S. (2006). The effect of alternate style keyboards on severity of symptoms and functional status of individuals with work related upper extremity disorders. *Journal of Occupational Rehabilitation, 16*, 707-718.

Sanders, M. S., & McCormick, E. J. (1976). *Human Factors in Engineering and Design* (7th ed.). New York: McGraw-Hill, Inc.

Schaefer, S., Lovden, M., Wieckhorst, B., & Lindenberger, U. (2010). Cognitive performance is improved while walking:

Differences in cognitive-sensorimotor couplings between children and young adults. *European Journal of Developmental Psychology, 7*(3), 371-389.

Smith, E. R. (2008). Seating. In K. Jacobs (Ed.), *Ergonomics for Therapists* (3rd Ed. ed., pp. 191-220). St. Louis , Missouri: Mosby.

Stubbs, D. A. (2000). Ergonomics and occupational medicine: Future challenges. *Occupational Medicine, 50*(4), pp. 277-282.

Svensson, H. F., & Svensson, O. K. (2001). The influence of the viewing angle on neck-load during work with video display units. *Journal of Rehabilitative Medicine, 33*, 133-136.

Swanson, N. G., & Sauter, S. L. (2006). A multivariate evaluation of an office ergonomic intervention using longitudinal data. *Theoretical Issues in Ergonomics Science, 7*(1), 3-17.

Thomsen, J. F., Gerr, F., & Atroshi, I. (2008). Carpal tunnel syndrome and the use of computer mouse and keyboard: A systematic review. *BMC Musculoskeletal Disorders, 9*(Retrieved from http://www.biomedcentral.com/1471-2474/9/134).

Tomei, G., Rosati, M. V., Martini, A., Tarsitani, L., Biondi, M., Pancheri, P., . . . Tomei, F. (2006). Assessment of subjective stress in video display terminal workers. *Industrial Health, 44*, 291-295.

Vieira, E. R., & Kumar, S. (2004). Working postures: A literature review. *Journal of Occupational Rehabilitation, 14*(2), 143-159.

Waersted, M., Hanvold, T. N., & Veiersted, K. B. (2010). Computer work and musculoskeletal disorders of the neck and upper extremity: A systematic review. *BMC Musculoskeletal Disorders, 11*(79), 1471-2474.

Wagner, F. (2005). *Easy Ergonomics for Desktop Computer Users.* CA: California Department of Industrial Relations.

Wahlstrom, J. (2005). Ergonomics, musculoskeletal disorders and computer work. *Occupational Medicine, 55*, 168-176.

Wu, C., Miyamoto, H., & Noro, K. (1998). Research on pelvic angle variation when using a pelvic support. *Ergonomics, 41*(3), 317-327.

Special Bonus

A resource you can use whenever you want.
Rather than simply listing all of my favorite books
and other resources here, I wanted to be sure
you had a link to a frequently updated selection.

Please visit www.NaomiAbrams.com to keep
working towards an injury-free life.

Don't want to do all that typing?
Put your Smartphone to work.
Scan this QR code to be taken directly to the Tip of the Month.

Made in the USA
Middletown, DE
10 February 2017